TANKMASTER

A practical guide to setting up your

COLDWATER
AQUARIUM

NICK FLETCHER

INTERPET PUBLISHING

2 0 0 4 3 6 3 7
MORAY COUNCIL
LIBRARIES &
INFORMATION SERVICES
639.34

Author

Nick Fletcher is a former editor of Practical Fishkeeping and still regularly contributes articles to this and other aquatic publications. His interest in tropical and coldwater fishes stems from his lifelong hobby of angling, which resulted in tanks containing several oddities, including pike. Nowadays, he prefers keeping fish to catching them, and is actively involved in koi circles at local and national level. Instead of a lawn he has a koi pond.

© 2000 Interpet Publishing,
Vincent Lane, Dorking, Surrey, RH4 3YX, England.
All rights reserved.
ISBN: 1-903098-06-8

Credits

Created and designed: Ideas into Print,
New Ash Green, Kent DA3 8JD, England.
Production management: Consortium, Poslingford,
Suffolk CO10 8RA, England.
Print production: Sino Publishing House Ltd., Hong Kong.
Printed and bound in China.

Below: One of the joys of a coldwater aquarium is being able to see the fishes behaving as they would in the wild. Here, the more colourful male stickleback entices a female towards the nest.

Contents

The colours of these fancy goldfish complement the decor in this aquarium.

Part One:

Setting up your aquarium

What is the attraction of a coldwater aquarium? A common reason for setting one up might be to revive childhood memories of goldfish in a bowl, but at a more sophisticated and responsible level. You could be forgiven for thinking that temperate species are easier to keep than their tropical relations; certainly, you will not run up such high heating bills. But warming the water is only a small ongoing cost. In reality, a coldwater aquarium offers its own unique challenges and rewards, and is in no way a poor relation of a tropical tank – it's just that bit different.

The first part of this book will show you how to choose and assemble a tank. Part Two covers alternative equipment, planting and decorative options, introduces you to some representative fishes and shows how to keep your aquarium in good order. But before you dash out to buy what you think you will need, tour your local aquatic outlets and find a dealer prepared to spend time to help you, the beginner, make the right choices. Better still, take along an experienced hobbyist friend, as they will know what to look out for.

The shop could be an independent retailer, part of a chain or a franchise attached to a garden centre – it does not matter, as long as the range of equipment is good, the staff knowledgeable and helpful, and the fishes healthy. Later, you may wish to specialise in fancy goldfish or some of the more 'exotic' coldwater species, but at this stage fish health is more important than pedigree.

Try to visit aquatic shops midweek, when business is fairly quiet and the staff will have more time to discuss your needs.

Good dealers will be cruel to be kind, so do not be upset if they refuse to sell you the fishes on the same day as you buy the hardware. They will know that rushing things is the sure-fire route to early failure – and losing a potential lifelong customer makes bad business sense.

Putting together all your purchases is covered step by step in the following pages. This should be a pleasurable exercise, so follow the steps slowly and carefully, and the end result will be an aquarium that is pleasing to the eye and provides a comfortable, long-term home for the occupants. Keeping fish is a responsibility. In a closed environment, they depend on you for everything. Keeping them healthy and seeing them respond to your care is the greatest pleasure your new hobby can offer.

What is a coldwater aquarium?

A coldwater aquarium is a setup that will support temperate fishes long-term without artificial heating. The species we are concerned with will survive within quite a wide temperature band, but are happiest midway between the upper and lower extremes. So while a common goldfish can live in water from near-freezing up to 30°C (86°F), it is best to aim for a minimum of 17°C (62°F) and site the tank so that it receives little or no direct sunlight that could raise the temperature significantly higher.

Consider installing a heater if the aquarium is situated in a room where the air temperature is likely to drop below the comfort level of the species you intend keeping. Even though the equipment may seldom, if ever, come on, this is useful insurance.

You will be spoiled for fish choice; there are more than 100 varieties of fancy goldfish alone, and a host of other suitable temperate species from all over the world. Several so-called 'subtropical' fishes, such as White Cloud Mountain minnows and the mosquitofish, will thrive in a slightly warm tank.

Keep within the law

Before buying (or collecting) any fishes native to Europe and the USA, check out the legal situation. In the UK, there is effectively a ban on keeping species that could escape and thrive in the wild, interfering with the indigenous fishes. These include bitterling, pumpkinseed and topmouth gudgeon. In the USA, interstate movement of some fishes is prohibited for much the same reason.

Fish tanks and children

The height of the tank from the floor is an important consideration, especially if there are young children who might run their wheeled toys into it. Stands and cabinets raise the tank to a good viewing height, but if you consider placing another aquarium on the lower level of one of the stands, be sure the location is childproof. This is as much for the safety of the child – who might inadvertently crack the tank – as the fish, should the child be 'helpful' and feed them (usually with a complete pot of food!) or, at worst, put undesirable substances into the aquarium.

Left: *Clear, rippling water, healthy plants and colourful, active goldfish are far removed from the traditional, but claustrophobic goldfish bowl.*

Above: *Stands are usually metal box section and supplied flat-packed. The trim at the top of the tank should match the colour of the stand and hood to help create a complete unit. A black baseboard below the tank makes a useful shelf.*

Standard tank sizes

You can buy all-glass aquariums in a range of standard sizes, in combinations of the following dimensions:

Length: *60, 90 or 120cm (24, 36 or 48in)*
Width: *30 or 38cm (12 or 15in)*
Depth: *30 or 38cm (12 or 15in)*

The tank and stand or cabinet that you choose will depend on how much you can spend, the available space and the fish you propose to keep. Bear in mind that the setup must fit in with your room decor and should therefore be both functional and attractive.

Avoid tanks that are very tall in relation to their volume. Within sensible limits, water surface area dictates stocking level more than total capacity. Be wary of complex geometric shapes, which can be difficult to position, illuminate and maintain. The best beginner's tank is rectangular, with height, width and depth all in proportion.

Modern tanks are made from glass sheets silicone-sealed together. The larger they are, the thicker the

glass must be. For example, a tank measuring 60x30x38cm (24x12x15in) should be made with panels 6mm (0.25in) thick siliconed onto a base 8mm (0.3in) thick. Tanks over 90cm (36in) long should incorporate one or more bracing bars.

Acrylic tanks have long been popular in the USA and are now gaining a following in Europe. They can be made in any shape, are extremely strong and do not scratch as ordinary plastic tanks once did.

Choosing a suitable stand

Powder-coated, metal box-section stands are ideal if you want to set up more than one tank; simply add a sturdy bottom shelf. Stands are sold flat-packed and slot together, though a mallet and a cushioning piece of board may be needed to persuade tight components to assemble. Use a lubricating oil spray on tight-fitting unions. A plain metal stand can look most attractive when the trim and shelf are colour-coordinated to the surrounding decor. Black ash, oak or teak are popular finishes. Do not try to economise by standing your tank on, say, a domestic table. A filled 68 litre (15 gallon) tank weighs more than 68kg (150lb), and most household furniture is not built to take that sort of weight without collapsing.

The trend today is towards a cabinet aquarium with integral hood (see page 31), but our main setup uses a separate hood unit.

Cabinets are available in natural or artificial wood veneer finishes, flat-packed or ready assembled. Depending on their design, they may have a lower cupboard and shelves for concealing wiring and equipment or storing food and accessories.

If space is limited, remember to take into account the total height of the stand and tank, as well as its width and length, and make sure there is enough room above it to carry out routine maintenance.

Sizes and capacities of standard tanks

Tank size (LxWxD)	Volume of water		Weight of water	
60x30x30cm (24x12x12in)	*55 litres*	*(12 gallons)*	*55kg*	*(120lbs)*
60x30x38cm (24x12x15in)	*68 litres*	*(15 gallons)*	*68kg*	*(150lbs)*
90x30x30cm (36x12x12in)	*82 litres*	*(18 gallons)*	*82kg*	*(180lbs)*
90x30x38cm (36x12x15in)	*104 litres*	*(23 gallons)*	*104kg*	*(230lbs)*
120x30x30cm (48x12x12in)	*109 litres*	*(24 gallons)*	*109kg*	*(240lbs)*
120x30x38cm (48x12x15in)	*136 litres*	*(30 gallons)*	*136kg*	*(300lbs)*

Filled, our 60x30x38cm (24x12inx15in) tank will contain about 68 litres (15 gallons) of water, weighing 68kg (150lb). And that is without taking into account the weight of the tank itself, the stand or cabinet, rocks and gravel. It is important to choose the right site, because once the tank is set up, it will be impossible to move without draining it down and wasting a lot of hard work.

A firm foundation

The floor must be able to support this considerable weight, particularly if the aquarium is sited in an upstairs room. If in any doubt, consult a structural engineer. The load-bearing capacity of a floor is greatest where it adjoins an outside wall, so in a bedroom it is unwise (and impractical) to make a centrepiece of the tank. Weight aside, there will be trailing electric cables to trip over.

Concrete flooring should safely support most tanks, although on carpet or vinyl tiles, it is advisable to spread the weight by placing a melamine coaster or flat piece of metal under each leg of the stand to prevent compression damage. If the setup must rest on floorboards, site the stand or cabinet so that the weight is transferred directly to the joists below.

The ideal position for a coldwater tank is out of the way of mainstream human traffic and away from

Right: Ideally, site the unit where it will not be affected by passing traffic through the room, light from windows and heat from radiators. Pick a secluded corner where you can easily install and service the aquarium.

Finding the best position for the aquarium

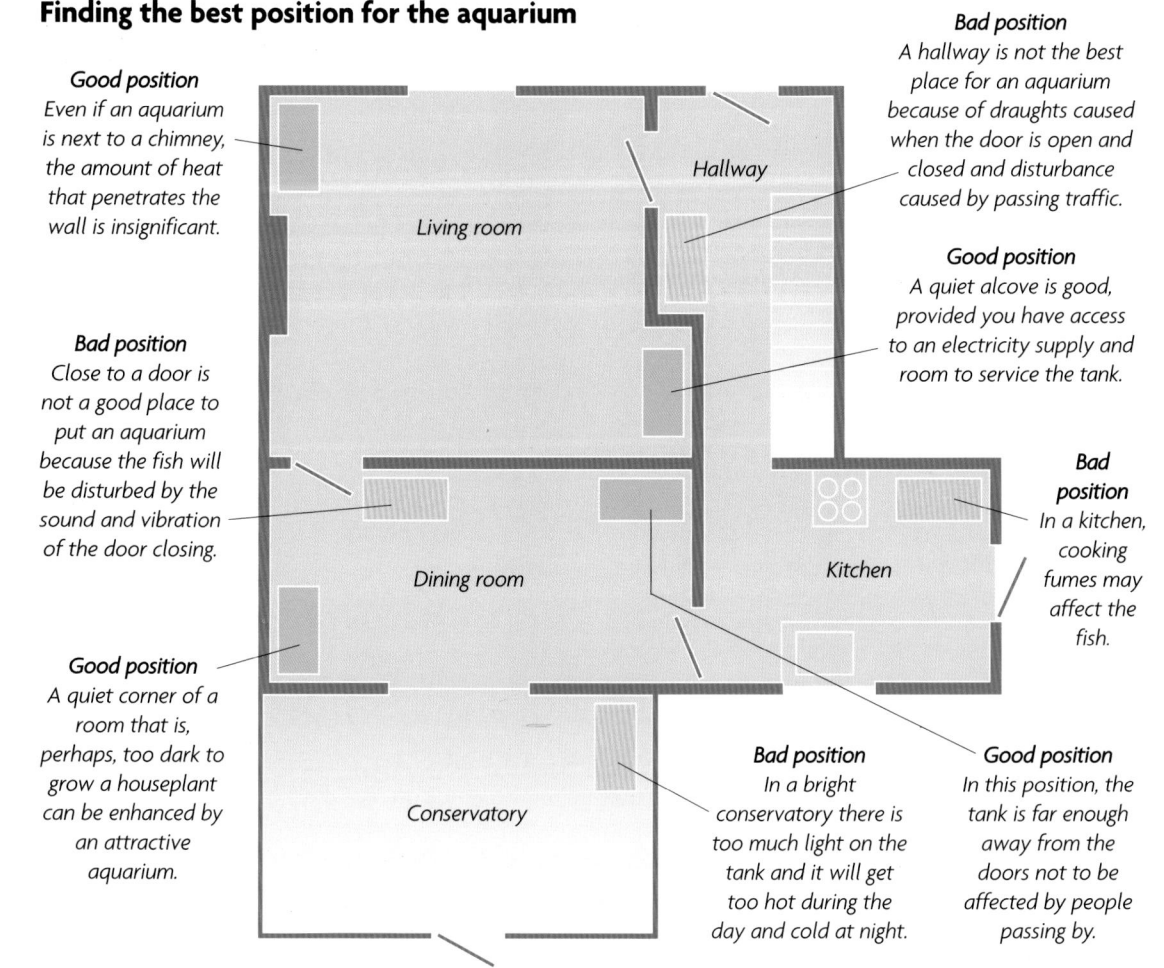

Good position
Even if an aquarium is next to a chimney, the amount of heat that penetrates the wall is insignificant.

Bad position
Close to a door is not a good place to put an aquarium because the fish will be disturbed by the sound and vibration of the door closing.

Good position
A quiet corner of a room that is, perhaps, too dark to grow a houseplant can be enhanced by an attractive aquarium.

Bad position
A hallway is not the best place for an aquarium because of draughts caused when the door is open and closed and disturbance caused by passing traffic.

Good position
A quiet alcove is good, provided you have access to an electricity supply and room to service the tank.

Bad position
In a kitchen, cooking fumes may affect the fish.

Bad position
In a bright conservatory there is too much light on the tank and it will get too hot during the day and cold at night.

Good position
In this position, the tank is far enough away from the doors not to be affected by people passing by.

Living room

Hallway

Dining room

Kitchen

Conservatory

doors, windows and radiators. It must be close to a power point and on a firm, level surface where it cannot tip or be pulled over. Avoid conservatories, as they receive too much light and vary in temperature with the seasons. Kitchens or workshops can contaminate the water with fumes or dust.

Take special care in houses with young children, particularly if you have two tanks on the one stand. Consider securing the stand to the wall behind with metal brackets, and fix a floor-level bump board about 10cm (4in) high to protect the lower tank from being cracked by children's toys or, indeed, the vacuum cleaner. Lock any cabinets to which children might gain access, otherwise the fish could be treated to a fatally large, although well-meant meal.

Choosing the right size tank

The tank we have chosen is a standard 60x30x38cm high (24x12x15in) with a separate hood and metal stand. This is really the minimum size to consider – large enough to provide a viable fish habitat, but small enough to find a place in most homes. The greater the volume of a tank, the less susceptible it is to sudden changes in temperature and water chemistry, and if anything does go wrong (such as filter failure), the trouble can usually be detected before irreparable damage is caused. Allowing 2.5cm of fish length per 150 sq cm (1in per 24 sq in), our 68 litre (15 gallon) tank, with its 1800 sq cm (288 sq in) of surface area, will support 30cm (12in) of fish.

Setting up the stand or cabinet and siting the tank on top requires time and space and preferably two people, since some items are awkward and heavy to manoeuvre. Sharing the tasks also prevents fatigue, which is when mistakes and accidents are most likely to occur. You need to work in a well-lit, uncluttered area, and have all your tools and equipment to hand

on a nearby table covered with a dust sheet – not on the floor, where you might trip over them. Switch off your mobile phone!

Stand the tank on a flat surface of carpet or polystyrene ceiling tiles while you attend to the stand. If it is supplied in a box or protective packaging, leave this in place for the moment. Assemble the stand or cabinet according to the instructions supplied. If wooden components require any gluing, allow the adhesive plenty of time to set. Now position the stand in its chosen location, double-checking that the power point is easily accessible and there is room behind for the plug or an RCD safety trip device.

Cabinets are self-contained, but metal stands will need a sheet of melamine-coated chipboard to support the tank. This should tap snugly into the top frame, with another one below acting as a shelf or a baseboard for a second aquarium. Carefully unpack the tank, checking for any obvious transit damage, and lift it into position, making sure that a sheet of polystyrene forms a cushion between the tank and stand. Ideally, this is a job for two people.

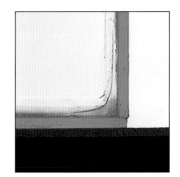

Left: An alternative to using polystyrene beneath the aquarium is a plastic foam sheet that evens out any irregularities in the stand.

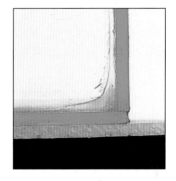

Left: As cushioning between the all-glass tank and its stand or cabinet, use a single sheet of polystyrene, cut slightly larger than the dimensions of the tank floor.

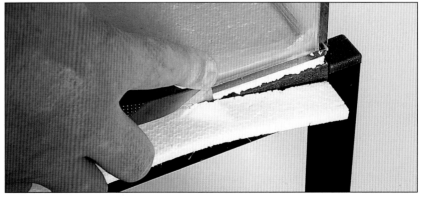

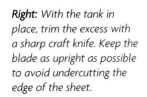

Right: With the tank in place, trim the excess with a sharp craft knife. Keep the blade as upright as possible to avoid undercutting the edge of the sheet.

A new aquarium may look clean, but it will have accumulated fine dust during storage. If this is not removed, it will leave a film on the water surface when the tank is filled. On tanks that have been shrink-wrapped or banded with tape, there may be unsightly sticky residues on the outer surfaces and the trim. Clean the glass inside and out, but avoid potentially harmful household chemicals.

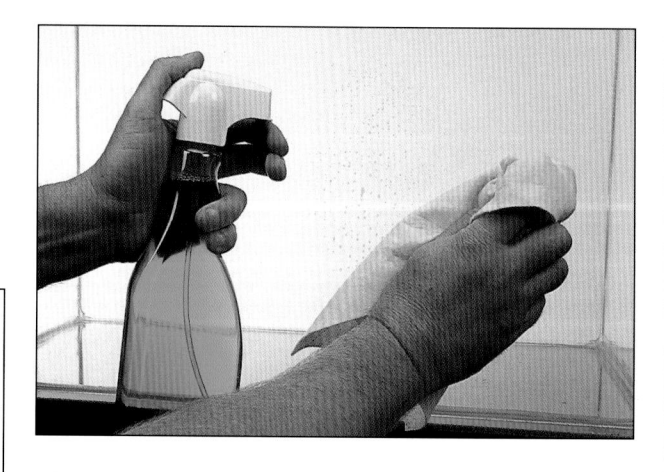

Above: *It is safe to use a non-abrasive spray cleaner on the outside glass, but inside, use only warm water on a clean, fluff-free cloth. Household chemicals will kill fishes.*

Making sure the tank is watertight

Fill the tank to the brim with mains cold tapwater to check for leaks. These rarely occur with silicone-sealed glass, but it is better to find out sooner, rather than later. Faulty new tanks will be under warranty, but if the tank is secondhand, drain it down and remove the offending strip of sealant with a craft knife. Thoroughly dry out the tank and clean the repair site with methylated spirit before resealing. Small repair tubes of silicone are available. Push, do not pull, the bead along the meeting point of the panes of glass, smooth off with a wet finger and then leave to cure for 48 hours. Thoroughly wash the inside of the tank again. If the tank is watertight, empty it before proceeding to the next stage.

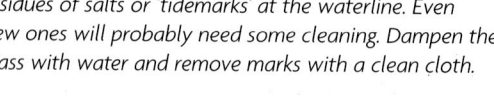

Above: *Secondhand tanks will almost certainly have residues of salts or 'tidemarks' at the waterline. Even new ones will probably need some cleaning. Dampen the glass with water and remove marks with a clean cloth.*

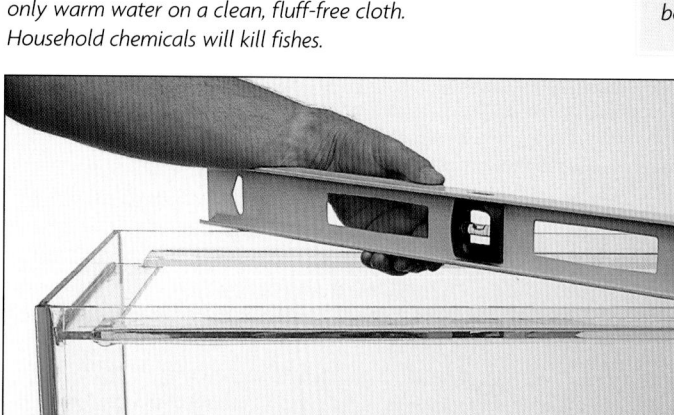

Left: *Use a spirit level from side to side and back to front to ensure that the stand is true. Test it again when the tank is in its final position.*

Making final adjustments

To compensate for uneven floors, metal knock-down stands have adjustable screw feet for levelling, as shown below. However, with cabinets you may have to pack under one or both edges with narrow strips of wood or cardboard. It is worth spending time at this stage making sure that both the stand and tank are absolutely level; mistakes are difficult to rectify later on in the setting up process.

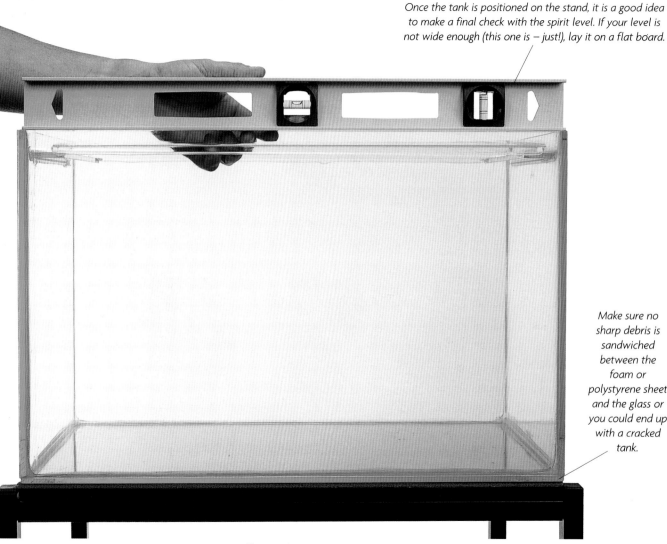

Once the tank is positioned on the stand, it is a good idea to make a final check with the spirit level. If your level is not wide enough (this one is – just!), lay it on a flat board.

Above: *Adjust the screw feet on each leg of the stand to ensure that everything is level. Ask a helper to hold the tank as you do this in case it is in danger of toppling over.*

Make sure no sharp debris is sandwiched between the foam or polystyrene sheet and the glass or you could end up with a cracked tank.

The material placed on the bottom of the tank, known as the substrate, is both functional and decorative. It can be naturalistic, mimicking a stream or river bed, or futuristic – anything from red river sand to coloured glass pebbles. But you must also consider the needs of the fishes and whether the substrate is going to play a part in filtration or act as a plant-growing medium.

Fish do not like substrates that are too pale. They reflect overhead light and make the tank occupants feel insecure. Dark material shows off their colours better; one dramatic scenario would be a bed of black gravel teamed with hard coal in place of the usual rockwork (see page 53).

Fine sand cannot be used over undergravel filters, as it falls through the slats in the plates and blocks the flow of water through the filter bed. At the other end of the scale, large fishes cannot easily dislodge coarse gravel, but uneaten food and other debris can lodge between the grains and decay.

For our purposes, substrates should be inert, which means they should not alter the chemical composition of the water. Always ask for lime-free gravel, and watch for any white fragments of calcareous material, such as shell, which could raise the pH reading too high in the aquarium (see page 26 for an explanation of the pH scale).

Do not collect your own gravel from river beds or beaches, as it may contain harmful metal ores or other chemical compounds.

Save money by buying aquarium gravel in bulk and sharing it among fishkeeping friends, or else store it ready for your next tank setup.

Coarse gravel/pea shingle
Best for large tanks, either on its own or mixed with medium grades to recreate the bed of a stream or rocky river.

Medium gravel (3-5mm/0.125-0.2in)
Available lime-free from aquatic shops and suitable for most setups. An ideal substrate for use with undergravel filtration.

Fine gravel (1-3mm/0.04-0.125in)
Ideal for smaller setups, where larger grades would look out of proportion to the rest of the decor.

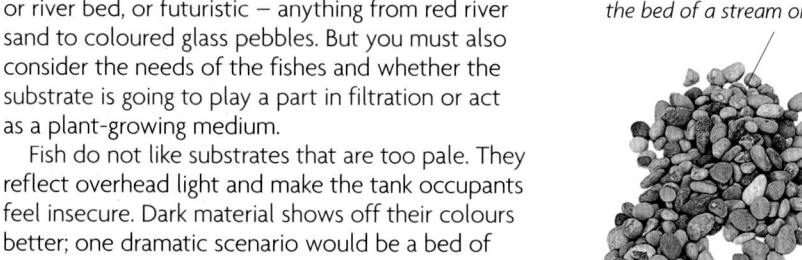

Black gravel
Fish swimming over a dark substrate show off their colours well. It can also be mixed in with lighter-coloured substrates to tone them down.

Polished pebbles in warm tones are decorative, but not a good filter medium because of their smooth surface.

River sand
These ultra-fine, water-worn rock particles with rounded grains do not damage the barbels of bottom-living fishes, such as loaches. River sand does not compact down and is highly suitable as a plant rooting medium.

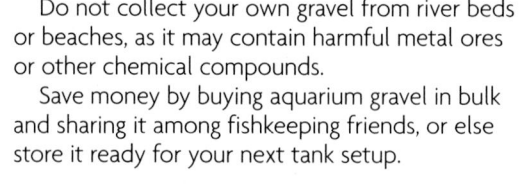

Coloured gravels
Buy these from a reputable source, otherwise toxic dyes could leach out, with fatal results. Available in single or mixed colours; avoid lighter shades.

Adding the gravel

Although sold as 'washed', aquarium sand and gravel still contain dust that you must first flush away. Working outdoors, half-fill a clean white or light-coloured plastic pail with the substrate and add water from a hose while stirring vigorously with a stick or wooden spoon. Keep tipping away the dirty water until it overflows clear. Small amounts can be rinsed over the sink in a plastic (not metal) colander.

Add the substrate in manageable handfuls or use a plastic measuring jug, taking care not to drop the gravel from a height.

How much gravel?

With an undergravel filter you will need a minimum depth of 7.5cm (3in). Other substrates should be deep enough for real or plastic plants, or to bed in rocks and wood decor; about 5cm (2in) should be enough.

Traditionally, the substrate is sloped from the back to the front of the tank. You may do this now as you spread it over the aquarium floor, but unless you put in rock or bogwood terraces to hold back the gravel, goldfish will flatten your artistic efforts as they dig around.

Using 'mature' gravel from a tank that has been running will help speed up biological maturation, but make sure it does not contain the small Malaysian livebearing snails with conical shells. These common pests are almost impossible to eradicate.

This setup incorporates an external power filter. It saves precious space within a relatively small aquarium, while offering a large volume of media to deal with the considerable waste generated by goldfish and other coldwater species. The unit is relatively bulky, but can be tucked out of view on the lower shelf or within a cabinet cupboard. It will require less maintenance than the much smaller, though still efficient, internal power filter.

Designs of external power filter vary between manufacturers, but the principle is the same in all cases. Aquarium water is drawn through the various media and pumped back into the tank. The intercepting media act in up to three ways: mechanically (extracting visible dirt particles),

This canister holds the media, and the motor unit makes a watertight seal with clips and an 'O' ring.

Inner container for media makes maintenance easier.

Filter wool traps waste particles. Do not pack it down too tightly or it may restrict the water flow.

The return pipe has a multi-directional flow control that allows you to direct the current in any direction you wish. Not all external power filters have this refinement.

The intake pipe draws in water through a strainer, which intercepts large particles of waste and prevents small fish being drawn into the filter.

All components, including the flexible piping and media, are included with this filter.

Multi-directional flow control

This grid fits on top of the inner container and prevents filter media being drawn into the impeller.

The motor unit drives an impeller to pull water through the filter and inlet and outlet pipe connectors.

Activated carbon is a chemical medium that removes chlorine and dyes from the water. Renew it regularly, as it soon loses its properties.

Clay pellets house beneficial bacteria. They never need renewing; just rinse them in aquarium water during filter maintenance.

biologically (breaking down harmful organic waste products) and sometimes chemically (removing other toxins and dissolved substances).

Lay out all the components so that they are to hand and check them against the instruction leaflet to ensure that none is missing, particularly small items, such as suckers. Remove the internal canister assembly and pack it with your chosen filter media. A coarse foam pad to trap large dirt particles goes in first, followed by a layer of ceramic pieces. These will later be colonised by beneficial bacteria. Tease out a handful of filter floss and lay this over the biomedia. You can then add activated carbon. Top this off with a final layer of floss. Fill the canister but do not compress the media down inside it.

Right: For ease of maintenance, pour the activated carbon into a bag formed from the toe of a nylon stocking or pair of tights. Make a loose knot in the bag.

Using a spraybar

A spraybar attached to the back glass with suckers is an alternative way of returning water from the power filter. The holes can be positioned to the rear to reduce turbulence. This return system is better suited to fishes that inhabit still or slow-moving waters in the wild.

Arranging filter media

In this model, water flows up through the media, first passing through the foam strainer pad. Other media can be substituted after this, such as aquarium peat to acidify the water, ceramic media, which do not easily block, or zeolite chips to bind in harmful ammonia when the tank is first set up. Avoid fine sand, which can pack down or find its way into the pump motor.

Filter wool sandwiches activated carbon.

Carbon can be added loose, but it is better to use a bag (see left).

Use only branded aquarium filter wool. Similar-looking materials can be toxic.

Pelleted biomedia house billions of good bacteria.

Wash the foam insert in tank water when it begins to clog with debris.

STAGE 5 Installing an external power filter

Place the canister within the outer plastic barrel and locate the pump motor – with inlet and outlet ports – on top. Check that the sealing 'O' ring is not distorted. Secure the motor with the integral clips. Do not force them. If they do not close easily, check that you have married up the components properly.

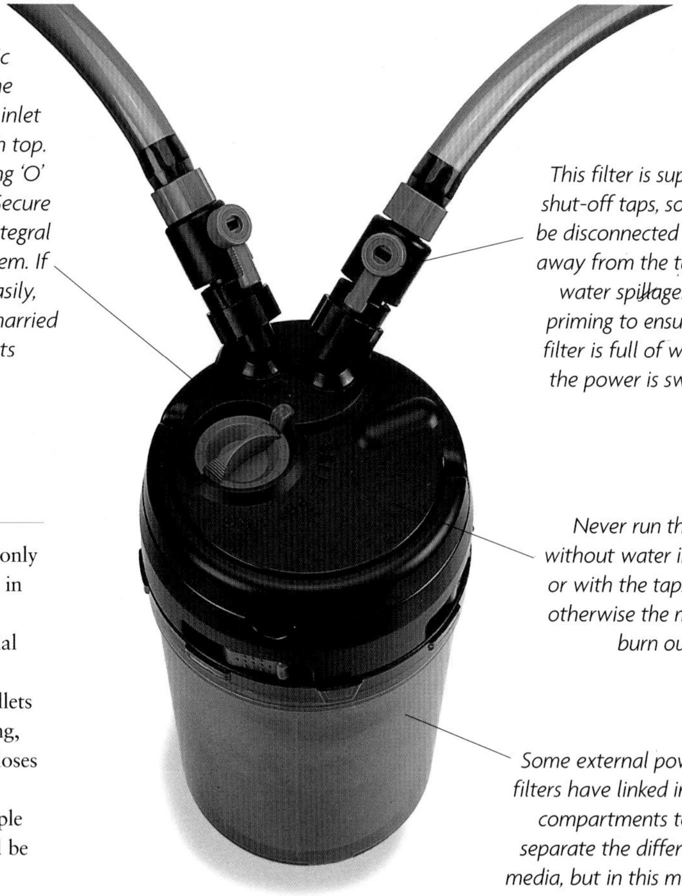

This filter is supplied with shut-off taps, so that it can be disconnected for cleaning away from the tank without water spillage. It is self-priming to ensure that the filter is full of water before the power is switched on.

Never run the filter without water in the tank or with the taps shut off, otherwise the motor will burn out.

Some external power filters have linked inner compartments to separate the different media, but in this model, the media are sandwiched between layers of floss to keep them apart.

Hints and tips

During maintenance, only ever rinse filter media in tank water to avoid killing off the beneficial bacteria they contain. Foam and ceramic pellets are virtually everlasting, but activated carbon loses its chemical filtration properties after a couple of months and should be replaced, as should inexpensive filter floss when it gets very dirty and begins to restrict flow.

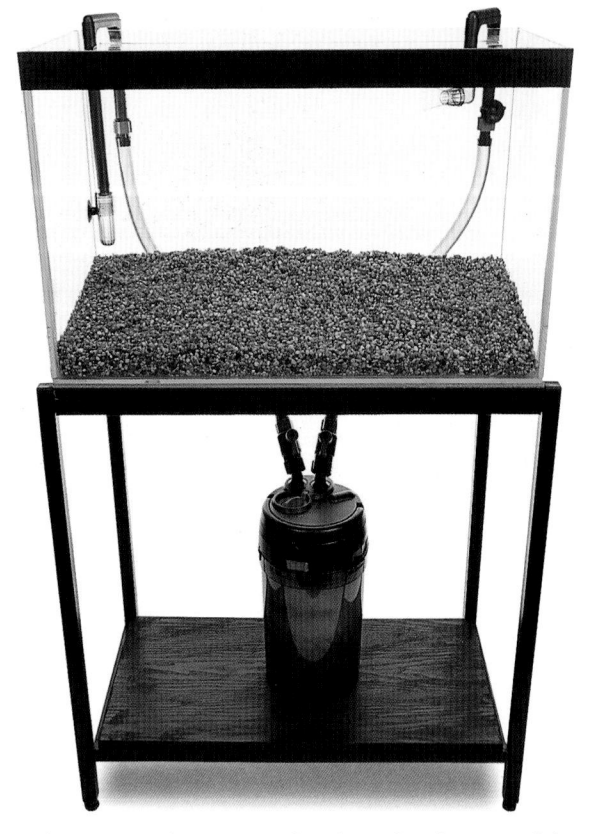

Above: *Screw the taps onto the inlet and outlet ports of the motor housing. Place the filter in its chosen position on the lower tank shelf or in the cabinet and connect the flexible hoses to the taps with the plastic locking nuts. Carefully measure the length of hose needed to reach the intake and return assemblies comfortably. Cut them both to fit and connect them up.*

Fitting the filter in the tank

Position the intake assembly in a rear corner of the tank. The strainer basket should be 1-2in (2.5-5cm) above the substrate, so that in the unlikely event of a pipe working loose, there will always be some water left for the fish.

The filter should turn over the total tank volume at least twice an hour, but this model will deal with an aquarium twice the size of this one. A larger filter will require less frequent maintenance and allows you to stock up to or slightly above the suggested maximum level in due course.

Position the return jet in the other rear corner, so that the flow is at, just above or just below the water surface. Fix it to the outside glass with the suckers provided.

Above: The intake pipe needs to pass through the aperture at the junction of the glass bars.

Above: To deliver aerated water back to the tank, use a multi-directional jet that hooks over the back glass.

A heater in a coldwater tank is not the contradiction it might appear. Although goldfish and other temperate species do not need the degree of warmth required by tropical fishes, a stable temperature is still essential to their well-being. This is usually provided in a centrally heated house during the day, but at night the domestic thermostat is often turned down, leading to a distinct fluctuation in tank temperature over a 24-hour period. This is not good for your fishes or any natural plants you keep with them in the aquarium.

With a heater installed, you have more control over the aquatic environment and a wider choice of fish species becomes available. If, for example, you wish to mix goldfish with White Cloud Mountain minnows (*Tanichthys albonubes*), you can arrange for the water never to cool below 18°C (64°F). In typical situations, the heater will rarely come on. A 100watt model will be quite adequate for a 60cm (24in) tank.

A further occasional use for a heater is when you wish to spawn your fishes. Some species are 'triggered' by seasonal rises and falls in the water temperature. (See page 66 for breeding.)

Hints and tips

Short power cuts are not usually a problem as far as heating goes. Your main concern will be loss of filtration. During longer periods of power failure, insulate the tank (including the hood) with blankets or sheets of polystyrene. For safety's sake, first switch off the lights in case the electricity supply is restored while you are away from the tank.

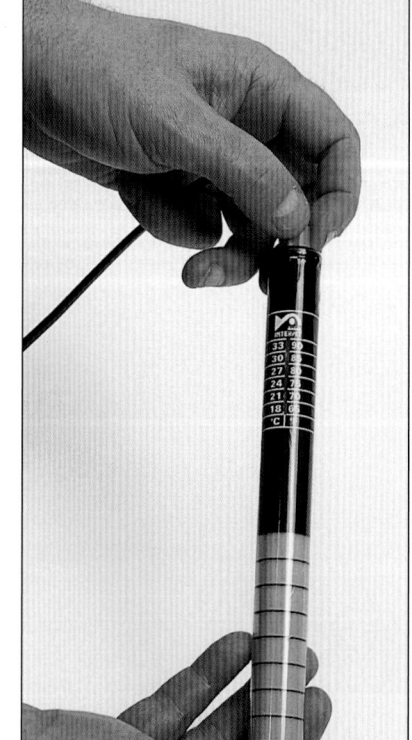

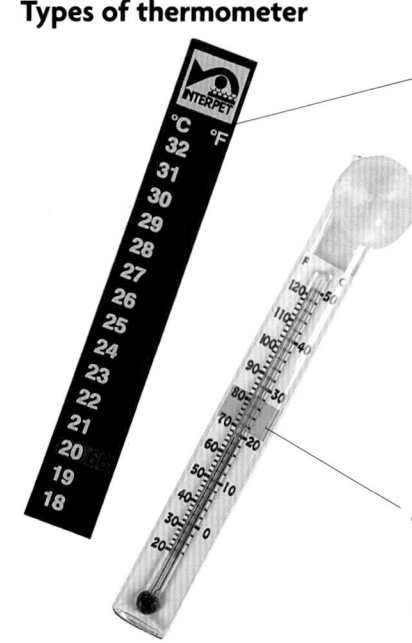

Types of thermometer

Digital thermometers stuck to the outside glass are popular, but they do not always give such an accurate temperature indication as more traditional types. Digital thermometers can be difficult to read under certain light conditions and are vulnerable to the attentions of children, who may try to peel them off.

Left: *Combined electronic heater/thermostats are housed inside the tank and are easy to regulate. They are factory set to about 23°C (73°F) and must be adjusted down in small, gradual steps until you achieve the right temperature. Do this well before you add any fish to the tank. If an 'on-off' light is included, make sure this is visible when the heater is installed.*

A good option is the in-tank alcohol thermometer that is held in place with suckers. The temperature readout can be the familiar vertical format or a dial with a pointer arrow. Either way, position the thermometer where it is easy to read at a glance, and make a habit of checking it every time you pass the tank. Boil-ups are rare with modern heater/thermostats, but it is better to be safe than sorry.

Installing the heater

Unpack the heater and read the instructions, as design and method of adjustment vary between manufacturers. Attach the suckers, set the temperature to the correct level and check this later against a reliable tank thermometer, making gradual adjustments up or down during a 24-hour period.

Safety first

If at any time you need to remove the heater from the tank, switch it off at least 20 minutes beforehand to give the element time to cool down. Never turn on the heater unless the tank is filled and the water level reaches the minimum specified on the unit.

▶ Hints and tips

Always carry a replacement heater and spare suckers to use in hospital/breeding tanks, or in the event of equipment failure.

Attach the suckers by sliding them along the body of the unit, so that one is near the top and the other near the bottom of the heater. You may need to wet them to stick them firmly to the glass.

Install the unit at an angle, not vertically, so that the rising heat does not directly pass the thermostat. The sensor should sample the ambient tank temperature, not a localised hotspot.

Leave a gap between the bottom of the heater and the substrate and never cover the unit with gravel, otherwise it will overheat. Similarly, do not obstruct water flow past the heater with any decor designed to conceal it.

Natural pieces of wood and roots make tasteful items of tank decor and are useful for concealing items such as airlifts. They can be used instead of, or as well as, rockwork to create a very informal effect or to provide refuges for light-shy fishes.

True bogwood is dug from peat deposits and consists of the roots or branches of oak or pine preserved in an acidic, anaerobic environment. The wood contains tannic and humic acids that you must remove by protracted soaking, otherwise they will leach into the aquarium water, staining it brown and lowering the pH level (making it more acidic). The 'younger' and paler the piece of bogwood is, the fewer contaminants it is likely to contain.

Varnishing aquarium wood with polyurethane to seal in contaminants will not work, as the varnish cannot penetrate all the natural crevices. Instead, trapped air will work under the varnish and lift it, giving the wood an unnatural silvery appearance.

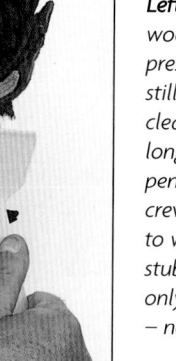

Left: *Shop-bought wood may have been presoaked, but it will still be dusty and need cleaning with a stiff, long-bristled brush to penetrate all the crevices. You may need to wet it to remove stubborn stains, but use only clean, warm water – no detergents.*

This piece of Mopani wood has a dark and a pale side, giving you the choice of two strikingly different decorative effects.

Each piece of natural bogwood is unique. This one has a gnarled, grainy appearance and the cracks could double as planting pockets.

Sand-blasted Mopani wood from the tropics is paler and heavier than bogwood and does not need presoaking.

Wood from the wild

Never collect wood from the wild, as it may be contaminated with pesticides or contain insects and their larvae. It will certainly carry fungal spores. Unseasoned wood will decay and pollute the water. Driftwood from the seashore is heavily impregnated with salt, and should also be avoided.

Small pieces of bogwood can look like jutting roots.

This medium-brown bogwood would look good positioned vertically. Try pieces at all angles for the best effect.

Adding the wood

Before buying any wood, hold it against a tank of similar size to your own to make sure that it will fit and is in proportion to the rest of the decor. One or two large pieces of the same type of wood create a better effect than several small ones. Choose interesting shapes without sawn edges or fine splinters.

If wood floats, weight it down in a bucket of water until it becomes waterlogged. This will also allow tannins to leach out.

Position wood horizontally to mimic fallen branches or vertically to resemble a tree trunk. Lay out the pieces dry before introducing them carefully into the tank. Push them well down into the substrate so that they cannot topple over. If they are still unstable, silicone seal them to a piece of slate and bed them into the gravel.

Heaters can be partially hidden by tall pieces of wood, but these must not touch the equipment or obscure the temperature indicator, if one is fitted. The same applies to power filters, whose intake and return must be unobstructed.

Tall pieces of wood, just like tall plants, look most natural positioned to the rear and sides of the tank. If you put a piece towards the front of the tank, fish can swim behind it and you will not be able to see them.

Why pay good money for rocks when you can pick them up almost anywhere for free? Apart from the legal consequences of helping yourself to other people's property, unless you are a student of geology you could be bringing in big trouble. The wrong rocks can alter water chemistry, particularly rocks based on carbonates, which raise the pH level (making the water more alkaline). Admittedly, this is not usually a great problem in a coldwater tank. Of more concern is the possibility that collected rocks could contain toxic metallic ores. Never use pieces of concrete, bricks or reconstituted stone.

The smooth contours of waterworn rocks look the most natural, with no sharp edges to injure fish. Igneous rocks such as granite are completely inert, but lack interesting shapes and texture. The Japanese volcanic rock known as Ibigawa, obtainable from bonsai outlets, makes a dramatic mountainlike centrepiece for any tank. Artificial lava rock is light and well-textured. Chunks of smooth, plain or coloured glass, or even well-cleaned antique bottles can substitute for rock-work (see page 53).

Washing rocks

Before use, scrub rocks thoroughly with plain warm water, paying particular attention to any crevices that could harbour organic matter. Secondhand aquarium rocks are usually discoloured where they have been partially buried or where algae has grown on them and they need especially vigorous treatment.

Slate is available in shades of dark grey, green or purple and can be bought in sheets or blocks. Take off any sharp corners with an abrasive wheel. This soft rock can be drilled and split. It is useful for shielding off the sides of the tank to give fishes a sense of security if there is a lot of passing human traffic.

Westmorland rock is a type of limestone, but fairly inert unless your aquarium water is very acidic. Waterworn pieces look best.

Do not collect pebbles and boulders from the beach or your local river. Most aquatic shops sell them quite cheaply.

Scattered slate pebbles create the illusion of a rock face that is being weathered and broken up.

Warm brown chunks of sandstone. Some types are too soft for aquarium use, so check first with your supplier.

Chunks of lava rock, although artificial, are not moulded but come in random shapes and textures.

Positioning the rockwork

Virtually every piece of rock has one face that is more interesting than the others. This is the one that should be visible in the tank. Long rocks can often look most effective if stood on end or at an angle. If you do this, silicone them to a wide slate base so that they cannot topple over.

*First position the main rocks, easing **them** firmly down into the substrate so that they rest on the tank floor. Then add the rest. Leave enough space for routine maintenance and make sure that none of the rocks or pieces of bogwood interferes with the working of filters or heaters.*

Group the larger rocks towards the back and sides of the tank. Odd-numbered groupings (three, five, seven, etc.) are visually more pleasing than even numbers.

Above: *Do not simply drop small pieces of rock onto the substrate. In nature, they would be part-buried and this is the effect we are aiming to duplicate. Small rocks need positioning with just as much care as larger ones, but at least they are easier to adjust later!*

Selected larger pieces of rock always look more natural than a scattering of smaller ones, although a few modestly sized accent rocks can set off the main pieces.

25

STAGE 9 Adding water – the vital ingredient

Goldfish are highly adaptable to variations in water chemistry and tolerant of a wide range of pH and hardness values. Other coldwater species are much less so, and it is better to find out the make-up of your local water supply and then match your livestock to it, rather than try to alter the water to suit their needs.

Depending on its source, the water will be acidic or alkaline, soft or hard. Use a reagent test kit or an electronic meter to measure pH and hardness. Water may also be seasonally polluted by nitrate and phosphate-based fertiliser run off from agricultural land. Sometimes the mains are flushed through with chemicals to remove shrimps and other bugs.

Heavy concentrations of the purifying gas chlorine can be smelled as water issues from the tap. Allowing it to stand in a clean container for 24 hours will dissipate the chlorine, especially if you use an airstone. Much more difficult to deal with is the chlorine/ammonia compound called chloramine, which can damage the gills of fish. Add a proprietary water conditioner to neutralise this chemical effectively.

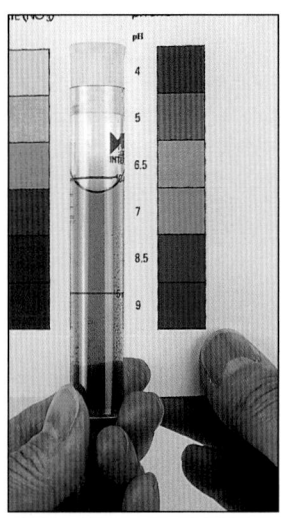

What is pH?

The pH value is a measure of water's acidity or alkalinity, expressed as the balance between hydrogen and hydroxyl ions. The more acidic the water, the more hydrogen ions will predominate and vice-versa. The pH scale runs from 0 (extremely acidic) to 14 (extremely alkaline), with neutral water at pH 7. However, because the scale is logarithmic, water of pH 5 will be 10 times more acidic than water of pH 6. Most coldwater fishes are happiest in stable conditions with a reading of pH 7-8.5.

Left: *You can check the pH reading of your water with the simple test shown here. Add a tablet to the water sample, shake the tube well and compare the colour change to a printed chart.*

How the nitrogen cycle works

All tanks undergo biological maturation. In new setups, the bacteria that convert harmful nitrogenous waste into useful plant nutrients are not yet established, but the moment you introduce any organic matter, ammonia will be produced. Fish excrete it through their gills during respiration and in their bodily wastes. This ammonia builds and peaks until Nitrosomonas bacteria multiply and begin converting it into nitrite. Another peak, this time of nitrite, occurs until the second line of defence, Nitrobacter bacteria, begin to take effect. Once these overlapping 'spikes' have levelled out (the time varies, but three weeks is the average), the only acceptable readings of ammonia and nitrite are zero, and nitrate should not exceed 50ppm (parts per million). Concentrations are kept down by real aquarium plants, which take up nitrate as a food, and by carrying out regular partial water changes.

Ammonia is excreted by fish through the gills and in their waste products.

Nitrates are taken up by the plants as a fertiliser.

Ammonia is converted to nitrites by bacteria in the filtration system.

Nitrites are converted to nitrates by bacteria in the filtration system.

Filling the tank with water

With the substrate, decor and electrical equipment in place, it is time to fill the tank. You can use cold or warm water, it does not matter at this stage.

Once you have introduced 7.5-10cm (3-4in) of water, you can speed up the process by slowly pouring from a clean, light-coloured bucket reserved for aquarium use. To prevent flooding, make sure the handle is securely fixed and steady the bottom of the bucket as you pour.

Fill the tank to 10cm (4in) below the final level, to prevent overflowing when you add the plastic plants.

Start by adding water from a clean plastic measuring jug onto a flat rock or a saucer if no suitable rocks are present. This avoids disturbing the prewashed substrate.

If you have cleaned the substrate properly, there should be very little clouding when the water is added to the tank. Wipe up any spillages and clean the inevitable drips from the outside glass. If allowed to dry, these can leave unsightly deposits.

Oxygen levels

Even if water is free from pollutants and of the correct chemistry, it must contain enough dissolved oxygen for the fishes to 'breathe', so never use distilled or purified water without heavily aerating it first or mixing it 50:50 with water from the tap.

If you keep fishes that like to dig around or snack on real plants, or you run your tank on undergravel filtration, artificial plants may be the answer. Another case for using plastic plants is that hoods on small tanks often have space for only a single tube, which may not provide enough illumination to maintain real plants in good health. You can also try a combination of real and artificial plants. Sensibly blended, it is quite hard to tell them apart.

Alternatively, plastic plants are available in fluorescent colours and futuristic shapes. They are not to everyone's taste, but they appeal to young children and are certainly a bit different.

Plastic plants are inert and virtually everlasting. Like the real thing, they will attract algae, which can be scrubbed off with a stiff toothbrush. They provide shelter and a spawning medium for fish, and their leaves and stems will be colonised by the same bacteria that live in the filter. But because they do not take up nitrates, as real plants do, you must pay extra attention to water changes.

Left: You can add or remove sections of plastic plants to vary their height, leaving the 'growing tip' in place for realism. Alternatively, buy different sizes of the same species and form them into clumps.

Convincing fakes

The quality of plastic plants varies greatly between manufacturers. Buy the best you can afford, as they will be with you a long time! When they first go into the aquarium, even the most realistic replicas can look 'too good to be true', but as the leaves acquire a fine coating of hair algae, the colours will be toned down. The most successful 'fakes' tend to be broadleaved varieties, such as Amazon swords.

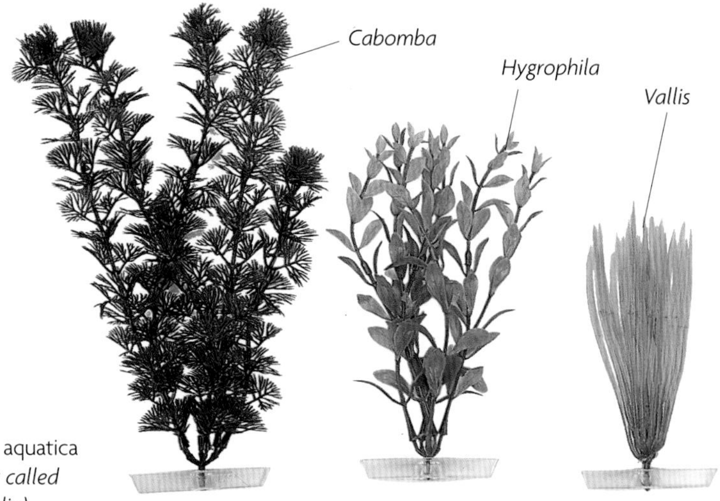

Cabomba

Hygrophila

Vallis

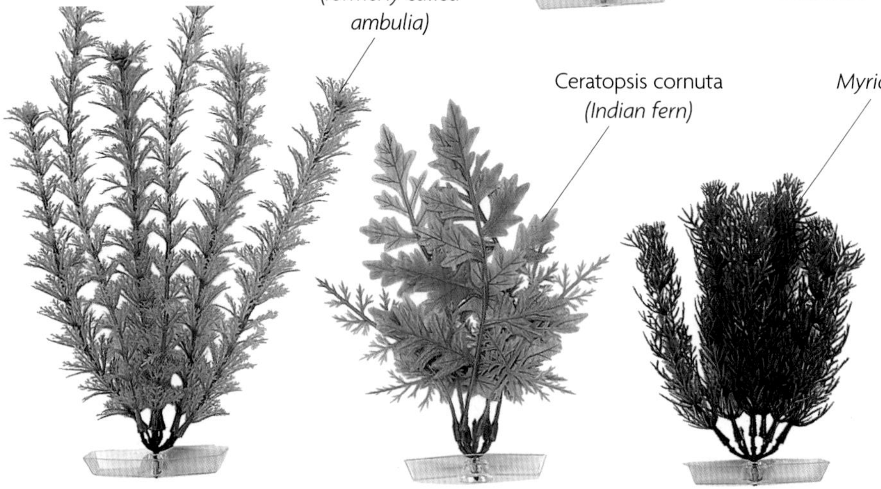

Limnophila aquatica (formerly called ambulia)

Ceratopsis cornuta (Indian fern)

Myriophyllum

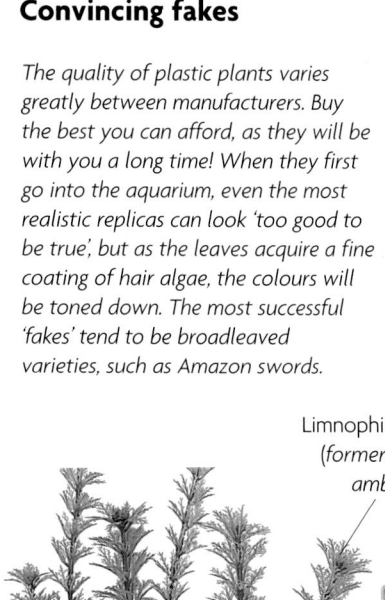

Enhance the realistic effect by mixing several different sizes of the same 'species' of plastic plant. Adding one or two large, tough-leaved, genuine plants will leave visitors wondering which are which.

Adding plastic plants

As with real plants, position the larger plastic examples to the back and sides of the tank, and keep smaller ones for the foreground. As there are no roots to damage, try each one in several locations until you discover which one looks best. Turn the plants until you find the most pleasing 'face'. Think where natural plants would be growing, including perhaps on bogwood or in the shelter of rocks where the current is not strong.

Above: *Plastic plants are anchored with plastic holdfasts, held in place by gravel. Slide these sideways into the substrate until they are fully concealed.*

▶ ### Hints and tips

Soaking the plants in near-boiling water or laying them on top of a radiator will make the plastic more pliable, enabling you to bend them into the shapes you want and iron out any crushing sustained in transit.

It is best to plant your tank before it is fully topped up, otherwise your hand and arm will displace water, causing it to spill out of the tank.

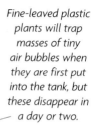

Fine-leaved plastic plants will trap masses of tiny air bubbles when they are first put into the tank, but these disappear in a day or two.

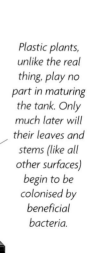

Plastic plants, unlike the real thing, play no part in maturing the tank. Only much later will their leaves and stems (like all other surfaces) begin to be colonised by beneficial bacteria.

An aquarium hood guards against fish escaping and prevents airborne dirt and dust from entering the water. It also houses the lighting that is essential for good, natural plant growth and, of course, enables you to view your fish.

Hoods are available in a number of styles, some matching the tank, others bought as separate units. In most integral hoods, the lighting tubes lie directly on a glass shelf, but in the aluminium type, the tube is secured with plastic clips and the starter unit sits on a shelf to the rear.

Modifying the hood

Before buying, check that the hood fits your tank and will accommodate all your equipment. A metal hood usually has slots to the rear to take cables and tubing, but it may need further modification, as here.

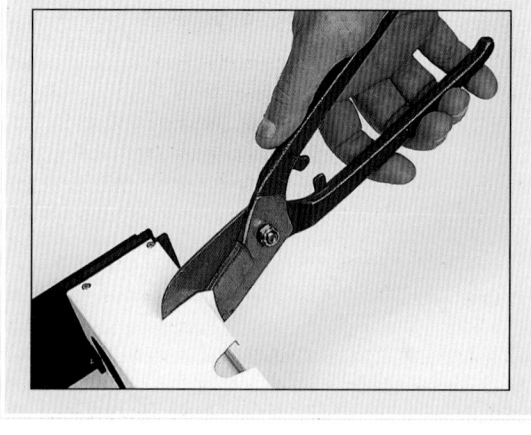

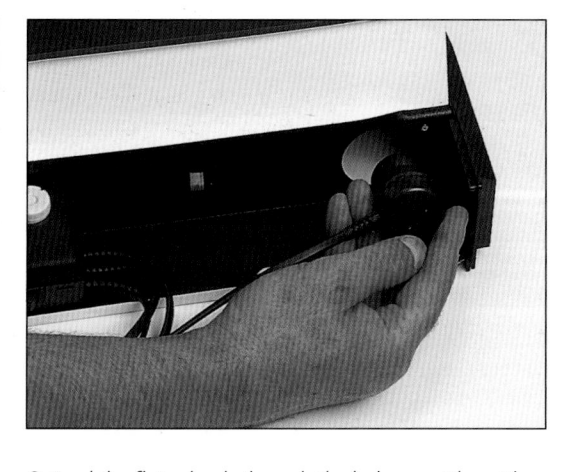

1 Position the starter unit on the shelf to the rear of the hood. Work well away from the tank, as this unit is quite heavy and would break the glass if it were dropped inside. Make sure it is not plugged into the electricity supply.

2 Feed the flying leads through the holes on either side of the shelf. Each end cap has two holes that correspond to the pins on the tube, and is shielded by a tight-fitting plastic collar to make a water-resistant union with it.

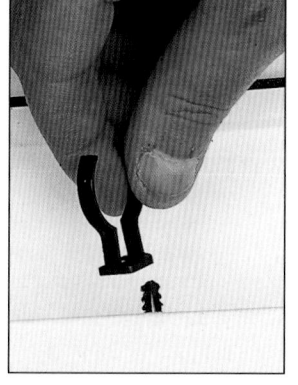

3 Fit the clips into the hood, using either the plastic nuts and bolts or self-tapping assemblies supplied. Do not over-tighten. You may need to drill holes in the hood or enlarge existing holes. Line up the clips ready to take the 15-watt fluorescent tube.

4 Line up the pins at either end of the tube with the holes in the end caps. Push the collars firmly home. Plug in and switch on the unit. If it does not work, try another tube before investigating fuses or the starter unit. Tubes are prone to transit damage.

Installing the lighting in the hood

Fluorescent tubes are the ideal beginner's choice. The various types imitate natural daylight, help promote plant growth and/or enhance the colours of the fish. If there is enough room in the hood, you can use more than one tube (for example, a white and a pink), but an ordinary warm white light is the best all-round choice if space is limited. Unless there are real plants in the tank, pick what best complements your fish and decor.

Ask somebody to hold up the front flap of the hood while you fit the tube, to prevent it falling onto your hands. Alternatively, tape it open.

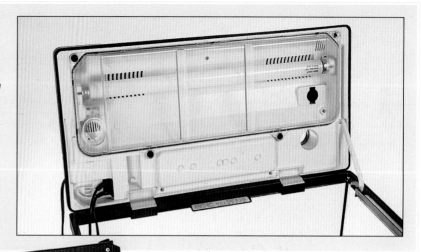

Built-in lighting

Some aquariums have custom-built hoods with an integral light fitting and a condensation tray, which protects the light tube from accidental splashes. The starter unit is concealed behind a separate panel. This is a neat, space-saving idea, but never rest anything on top of the tank, as these units need to be well ventilated.

Align the tube centrally and gently push it into the retaining clips. Do not use force or you may break them.

Boosting the light

If the design of the hood allows, consider installing a reflector over the tube. This will direct all the light down onto the water, boosting the efficiency of the light.

STAGE 12 Fitting the condensation tray and hood

The condensation tray is located between the hood and the water surface, where it cuts down evaporation losses and prevents damp reaching the light fittings. It also stops fish jumping out of the aquarium. Tanks with integral hoods often have clear cover glasses that can be slid aside for feeding or maintenance, doubling as a support for light tubes.

In this setup, we are using an inexpensive alternative, a plastic condensation tray. Using a damp cloth, regularly clean both types of tray of dust, salt deposits, algae and fish-food particles, so that light can fully penetrate the water (see page 70).

Condensation trays are available in sizes to match standard tanks, but you will need to modify them to accommodate equipment and allow fish to be fed.

Allow access for feeding

Do not forget to cut a hole in the front of the condensation tray as well, to allow you to feed the fish. Some people prefer this to be positioned centrally, others feed at one corner – it does not matter which. You must also make an aperture to allow the free passage of food from an autofeeder, should you decide to install this convenient piece of equipment (see page 65).

Right: *Flexible plastic covers are easy to trim with scissors. Cut the rear corners diagonally, ensuring that there is space for the heater and filter cables and external power filter intake and return pipes. It is best to take off a little material at a time, as you cannot put it back once cuts have been made!*

Above: *Position the modified tray over the glass ledges, with the moulded depressions facing down. If necessary, trim one or more edges so that it fits snugly without any buckling.*

Fitting the hood

With the plants and decor in place and the life-support system up and running, it is time to marry up the assembled hood to the tank.

The hood must fit flush and level all round the tank and not trap any pipework or cables. Check that the front aperture opens and closes freely. The recessed handle is sometimes difficult to open with wet hands. A glass marble, silicone-sealed in place, provides a much better grip.

Right: With their trailing cables, hoods can be quite heavy and awkward to manoeuvre single-handedly, so enlist some help if possible. Otherwise, temporarily secure the starter unit to its shelf with strong tape and do the same thing with the mains lead and plug.

The condensation tray should lie flush on the glass bars and not obstruct the hood as it is lowered into place.

Make a final check of the tank layout. Minor adjustments are easier to make before the hood goes on.

Decorative plastic backgrounds behind the tank conceal electric cables, filter pipework and the wallpaper, adding to the overall visual appeal of the aquarium. They are sold off the roll or to an approximate size, and are easy to trim with scissors. The design you choose is a matter of taste; a planted underwater scene, tree roots, rockwork or classical temples are all popular.

Trim backgrounds with care
You can trim the simulated rockwork background at any point without disrupting the effect. Other designs require more thought, so that you do not lose the tops off simulated underwater plant thickets or the boles of tree roots.

Right: Cork floor tiles glued to the outside of the back glass create a good neutral effect. The tiles can be used straight from the pack or roughly scored to suggest a rockface.

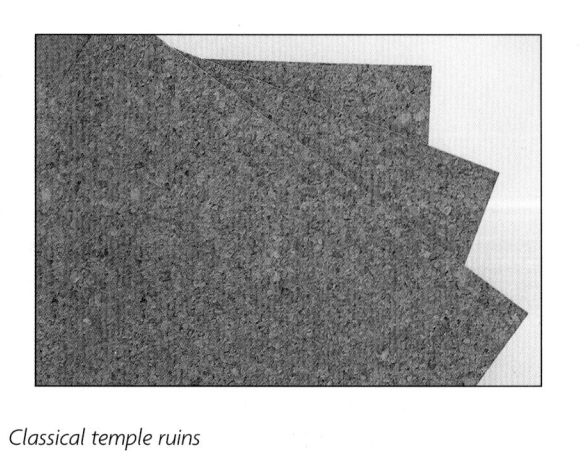

Above: Stretch the background tightly across the outside back glass and hold it place with two vertical strips of clear adhesive tape. (Using a tape dispenser makes the job much easier.) Make sure the glass is completely dry, otherwise the tape will not stick. At this stage, you may need to cut slots or pierce holes in the background to accommodate suckers for power filter intakes or outlets.

When in doubt, a plain black background is a safe choice. The graduated blue option on the other side tends to make tanks look cold.

A background mimicking plants and rocks is fine, as long as your tank features these elements, too.

Classical temple ruins could form a credible background if your tank contains ornaments in the same style.

This rock background gives a realistic 3-D effect and it does not matter whether it is trimmed from the top or the bottom.

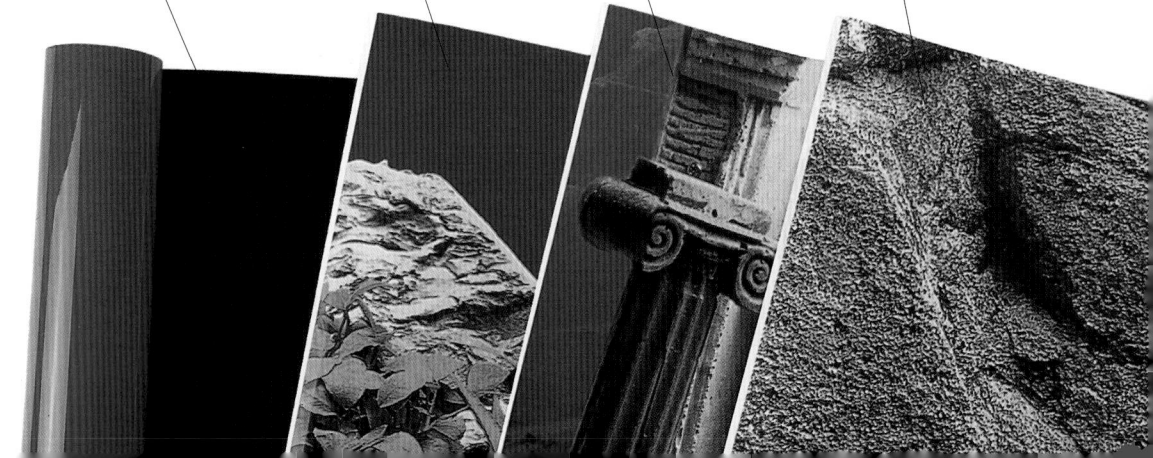

Maturing the tank

With the tank complete, the great temptation is to rush out and buy the fish. Resist it! Self-restraint is needed while the filtration system matures biologically, which will take up to six weeks. And if you have real plants, these will need to establish their root systems without disruption. Leave the lights on for 10-14 hours a day to promote healthy growth. A timer switch is a good idea if you are away from home a great deal. After two weeks, carry out a nitrite test (see page 71), and if the reading is acceptable, you can add your first fish. Test daily after this and if the nitrite level creeps up again, carry out a partial water change. Add the rest of the fish gradually over the coming weeks. This way, you will avoid the common problem of 'new tank syndrome (see page 69)'.

In time, the gravel surface will become home to colonies of nitrifying bacteria. The effect is greatly enhanced if an undergravel filter is used, but all available surfaces within the tank will eventually play a small part in biological filtration.

In a tank containing real plants, there will be some organic matter to start off the colonies of beneficial aerobic filter bacteria. Our tank has only plastic plants, so it is relatively sterile and must be seeded either with a small daily pinch of flake food or a proprietary bacterial culture. However, neither of these is a substitute for patience.

Above: *Now you can install the thermometer. This internal type is held in place with a single sucker in a top front corner of the tank, away from the current of the power filter. It is easy to reposition or remove if you want to monitor the temperature during water changes.*

Take your time choosing your first fishes. They should be with you for quite some time, so buy specimens that appeal to you. Once the dealer has netted them into a plastic bag, hold them up and examine them from all angles to make sure they are healthy, with no split fins, deformities or ulcers. Pay special attention to the belly area, which is easy to overlook but often the site of infection.

The bag containing the fishes and a small amount of water is inflated with oxygen and sealed with an elastic band. Sometimes, dealers will add a stress-relieving chemical. Ask them to tape up the corners of the bag, so that small fishes cannot become trapped and damage themselves.

Left: Once you are home, gently remove the outer wrappings. If the trip has been short, float the sealed bag in the tank to equalise the water temperatures.

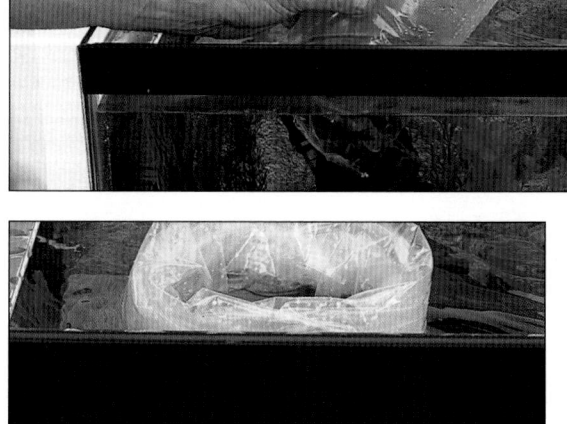

Left: For the journey home, place the plastic bag into a brown paper outer or black bin liner to help keep the occupants calm. On long journeys, stand the bag upright inside an insulated polystyrene box. Hold it in place with balls of newspaper. Go straight home; the less time the fish spend in transit, the better they will cope.

Above: Following a longer journey, open up the top of the bag to dispel the stale air. Roll down the sides to form a collar. Leave the lights off, as they will only stress the fish. After about 20 minutes, check the water temperature by dipping a finger into the bag and then into the tank. You will be able to tell if the fishes are ready to be released.

Above: Be gentle when transferring the fishes from the bag to the tank. Turn the bag on its side and hold it open with one hand while you gently tip it with the other. Give the fish plenty of time to swim out. Make sure they all do, and that none is trapped in the rolled-down collar. Carefully dispose of all used plastic bags straightaway.

The completed setup

When all the fish are in the tank, carefully replace the condensation tray and hood and leave the fish to settle down for a further 30 minutes. You can then return to switch on the light and admire the finished aquarium.

Heavy early feeds will only overload the filtration, so wait until the following morning before adding a very small amount of flake or tablet food. You will be surprised how fast fishes learn to feed from the hand.

Fish that hang close to the surface are either sick or the victims of bullying. If you lose one individual soon after stocking, do not panic – it happens – but always try to pin down the cause.

The fish will probably not yet be swimming in open water, but hiding among the plants or behind rocks and wood. Nor, due to stress, will they be showing their best colours, but never fear, this is normal. Do not offer food to tempt them out. They will emerge in good time when they have gained confidence.

Long-finned fancy goldfish are occasionally the target of fin-nipping shubunkins. You may have to return the culprits to the shop where you bought them or move them to another tank.

Setting up a hexagonal aquarium

This 60cm (24in) tall hexagonal aquarium is a viable alternative to the traditional rectangular tank. It occupies little floor space and holds approximately 82 litres (18 gallons) of water. Such a compact tank can easily become cluttered with equipment, so this one will contain just a small internal power filter and an (optional) heater/thermostat. Fluorescent tubes would be difficult to install in the simple plastic hood supplied and would not give sufficient light penetration down to the substrate. As the intention here is to use natural plants, we shall opt instead for a 125-watt mercury vapour lamp, suspended 30cm (12in) above the water surface.

A stress-free environment

Six-sided tanks are sometimes placed in the middle of a room to give an all-round view of the fish, but such exposure will stress the occupants. It is much better to position the tank against a wall, where it is less likely to be knocked over. If you tape an external background to the three rear panels, the fish will feel even more secure and show themselves at their best.

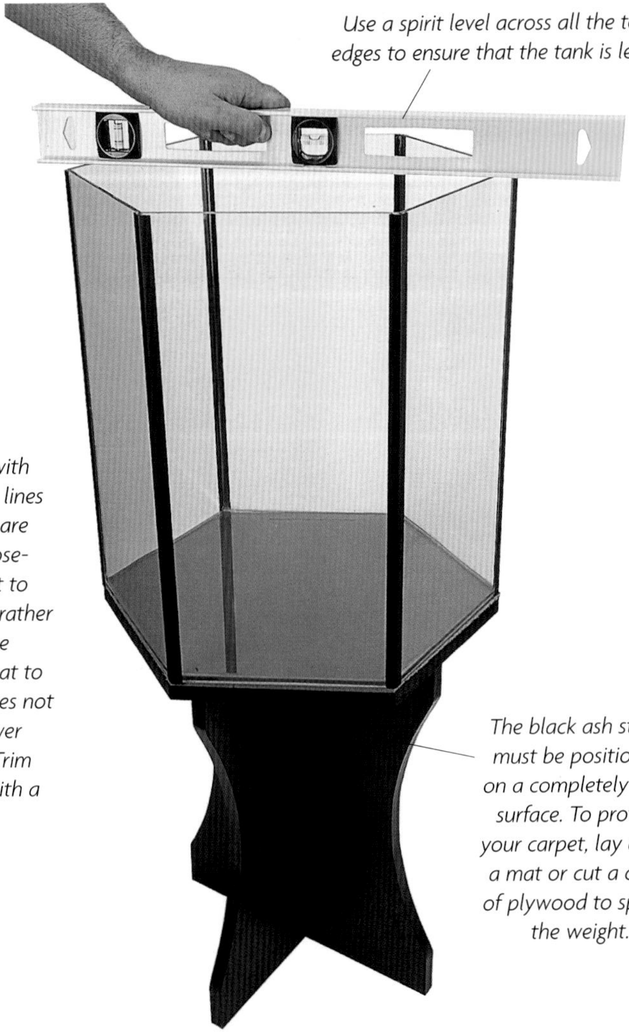

Use a spirit level across all the top edges to ensure that the tank is level.

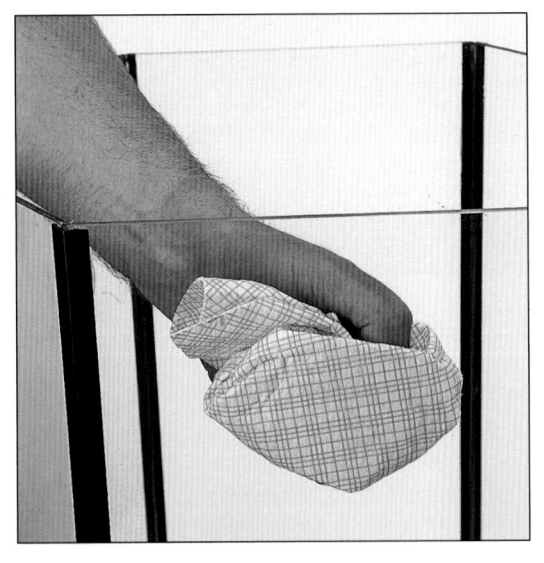

Right: Carefully unpack the tank and start by cleaning the glass inside and out with a damp cloth. Rest the tank on a carpeted floor while you do this and steady it with your free hand so it cannot tip over.

Right: In keeping with the clean modern lines of this design, we are using a thin purpose-made flexible mat to cushion the tank, rather than a polystyrene sheet. Tape the mat to the stand so it does not slip when you lower the tank onto it. Trim excess material with a sharp craft knife.

The black ash stand must be positioned on a completely level surface. To protect your carpet, lay down a mat or cut a circle of plywood to spread the weight.

The substrate here is a lime-free river gravel with fine rounded grains. A coarser material would look out of place in a small tank like this, and would not be an ideal rooting medium for the plants.

Wash the gravel thoroughly before use. Place a few handfuls at a time into a clean, light-coloured plastic bucket and agitate it with your hand or a wooden spoon under a running tap. Periodically, tip away the dirty water and refill the bucket. Take your time; there are no short cuts, but patience will pay dividends. With a light-coloured bucket it is easier to see if the water is clear.

Add the washed gravel in handfuls or, as here, from a plastic measuring jug, until it forms a 3-4in (7.5-10cm) layer on the tank floor.

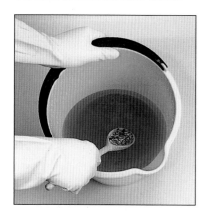

There is less likelihood of damage to the tank base if you allow the first jugful of gravel to form a pile and continue to build it up.

Above: *Slope the gravel down roughly from the back to the front of the tank. If you need a heater, position it with suckers on the rear panel, well above the substrate, at a 45° angle.*

Installing an internal power filter

Internal power filters are ideal for small aquarium setups. They strain the water of suspended particles and, more importantly, act biologically to break down pollutants into harmless compounds that natural plants take up as nutrients. Additionally, they create circulating currents that help with the oxygenation of the water. Some internal power filters have a compartment for activated carbon, a chemical medium that is especially useful when a tank is first set up.

The filter support frame fits into 90° corners, but cannot be used in a hexagonal tank with 120° angles between the panes.

An open-cell foam cartridge is the main filter medium.

Above: Cut the filter foam insert into two. This will enable you to rinse the pieces in rotation, so that there will always be a healthy population of beneficial bacteria within the filter.

Motor unit with impeller chamber to power water through the filter.

The filter support frame is held in place with suckers. Moisten these before pushing them onto the glass. (We will not be using this frame in the hexagonal tank.)

Tubing for optional venturi, which draws air bubbles into the filter outflow.

Multidirectional water flow control.

Compartment to hold activated carbon granules.

Activated carbon granules remove any brown tints leaching into the water from bogwood decor. Renew this material every month or two.

40

Motor/impeller unit.

As fitted here, the flow control will direct the water downwards.

Chamber for activated carbon.

Foam insert slides into filter canister.

Right: *Place the filter as close as possible to the back panel without touching the heater/thermostat. It can safely rest on the substrate, as the canister does not draw in water from the bottom.*

Right: *The components of the filter push-fit together. Read the instructions carefully to ensure that everything lines up and never use force.*

Hints and tips

In a hexagonal tank you can achieve very good water circulation. Direct the flow from the internal power filter so that it plays across tall plants, imparting gentle movement, but do not aim it directly towards the front glass. Leave enough room to remove the filter for cleaning without disturbing hard decor.

Providing the materials are inert and non-toxic, hard decor is very much a matter of personal choice. Some people like underwater castles and air-powered ornaments, but as this is a planted tank, the aim is to create a natural effect.

Tall items are most in keeping with this hexagon, drawing the eye upwards and helping to hide the equipment. With limited floor space, it would be easy to clutter the setup, so keep the decor towards the back, allowing plenty of room for the plants.

We are using lava rock and prepared bogwood, a very hard and dense natural material that will not leach tannin into the water. However, both still require a thorough wash before going into the tank.

Falling midway between natural and novelty items of decor are convincing casts of actual rocks and stones in resin. Some are hollow, providing refuges for fish. Once they have been installed for a while they are indistinguishable from the real thing.

Roofing slates, stood on end against the back glass, function like artificial backgrounds, giving the fish a sense of security in the tank. They can be shaped with a file to remove sharp edges and the result is an attractive, rounded profile.

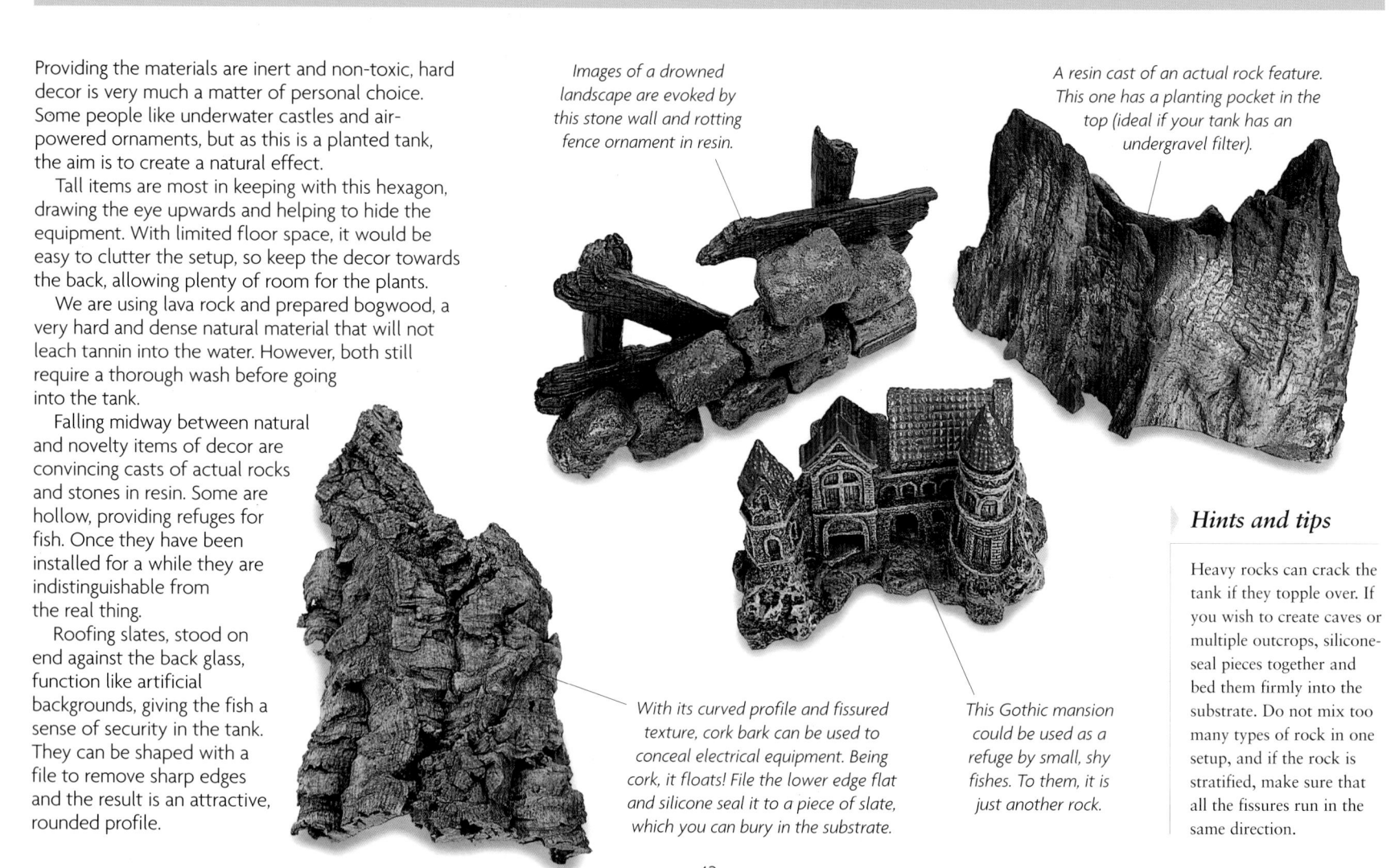

Images of a drowned landscape are evoked by this stone wall and rotting fence ornament in resin.

A resin cast of an actual rock feature. This one has a planting pocket in the top (ideal if your tank has an undergravel filter).

With its curved profile and fissured texture, cork bark can be used to conceal electrical equipment. Being cork, it floats! File the lower edge flat and silicone seal it to a piece of slate, which you can bury in the substrate.

This Gothic mansion could be used as a refuge by small, shy fishes. To them, it is just another rock.

Hints and tips

Heavy rocks can crack the tank if they topple over. If you wish to create caves or multiple outcrops, silicone-seal pieces together and bed them firmly into the substrate. Do not mix too many types of rock in one setup, and if the rock is stratified, make sure that all the fissures run in the same direction.

This prepared bogwood has a tapering root that will lie diagonally across the foreground gravel, enabling a small terrace to be created behind it. The resulting planting pocket will look very natural. Note how the filter is all but concealed.

At this stage, too much gravel is visible against the front panels, but final adjustments can be made as the plants are added.

Above: Offer up the first piece of lava rock, making sure the most attractive face is visible. You will probably need to make several adjustments: positioning the decor is critical in such a small tank, as it will not be easy to make changes once the plants are introduced.

Right: To get the necessary height, you may need to pile rocks on top of one another. With irregularly shaped pieces like these it is quite easy to set them up firmly, but smooth rocks should be siliconed together over a wide base piece so they cannot topple over and crack the glass.

Adding the water and plants

A surprising number of plants sold as 'tropical' will thrive equally well in tanks at room temperature. These include vallisneria, egeria, myriophyllum and hydrocotyle. But check their suitability with your aquatic dealer, as similar-looking species can have very different temperature requirements.

For best results, plant taller specimens to the back and sides of the tank, and more compact varieties towards the foreground. Leave areas of substrate clear at the front for the easy removal of debris. Bunched plants are held together with a padded lead strip. In a confined space such as this, leave the lead in place and simply wriggle the whole bunch into the gravel. The lead will not pollute the water.

Right: *Floating plants, such as Salvinia auriculata, diffuse light and cast attractive shadows down through the water. This species reproduces quickly from side shoots, but can be easily thinned out.*

The straplike leaves of Vallisneria natans conceal equipment and make a delicate backdrop to the tank decor.

Egeria densa soon forms dense clumps to the sides and rear of the setup.

Establishing plants

With the lights and filter running, allow plants at least two weeks to root and establish themselves before introducing the fish. Plants will also help to stabilise the tank biologically, but keep first fish stockings low, test the water and carry out regular partial changes until filter bacteria have built up.

Below: Pour water onto rocks or bogwood to avoid displacing the substrate. Fill only threequarters full to avoid overflowing as you introduce the plants. Let it stand for 24 hours to dissipate chlorine, then take the chill off it by adding water from the hot tap.

The tallest leaves of vallis may need trimming back, but wait until the tank is completely filled.

Right: Start at the back of the tank and work forward. When planting pennywort, as here, remove it from its small pot of rockwool and push individual stems into the gravel.

Above: Plant myriophyllum into the substrate complete with its lead strip weight. New roots will soon emerge above the lead to anchor the clump.

Above: Just drop salvinia onto the water surface. The plant is self-righting, with water-repellent leaves! It spreads quickly and will need thinning out.

45

Introducing the fish

Goldfish are renowned plant eaters, so for this small planted tank a good choice is a mixed shoal of White Cloud Mountain minnows *(Tanichthys albonubes)*, including both the normal 'wild' form and fish bred to show more red. A long-finned variety is also available.

These fish are hardy and inexpensive, and swim actively at all levels in the water, darting in and out of the plants and playing in the return from the power filter. Their colours are enhanced by the overhead mercury vapour lamp. Allow the plants 10-12 hours of light a day.

Settling in

Once the fish are in the tank, leave them to settle down for an hour or two with the lights off, and do not offer food until the following day. Initially they will hide away and exhibit faded colours, but this will soon pass as they gain confidence and begin to explore their new home with enthusiasm.

Below: *With the light on, the full beauty of the White Cloud Mountain minnows becomes apparent.*

Above: *Roll down the neck of the bag to form a floating collar and, with the lights out, allow temperatures to equalise. After 20 minutes, mix in small amounts of tank water.*

Above: *Gently tilt the bag, holding the neck open, and allow the fish to swim free of their own accord. Make sure no fish are trapped in the folds of the bag; they are easy to miss!*

The completed tank, topped up and lit from above. Floating salvinia softens the waterline.

Mixed plantings of vallisneria, egeria and hydrocotyle contrast well with the rugged texture of the lava rock and bogwood, and provide valuable cover for the fish.

The plain black background taped to three rear panels hides the wall behind the tank and brings out the colours and textures of the aquascaping.

Right: With about 12 hours of lighting daily and small fish fed only sparingly, this tank will require little time spent on maintenance, other than glass cleaning, regular partial water changes and the removal of dirt from the open area of substrate at the front.

Above: Take professional advice on installing the heavy mercury vapour pendant lamp. There will be more evaporation than in a covered tank, so keep a supply of aged top-up water to hand.

A brightly coloured male shiner (Notropis lutrensis) *escorts his chosen female.*

Part Two:

Options and ongoing care

By this time, you should have a fully functional coldwater aquarium up and running. The equipment we have chosen is very efficient, but there are several other equally rewarding ways in which it is possible to approach the project. In this part of the book we look at other options involving filtration and decor, and we also feature more plants suited to a coldwater aquarium. You may wish to consider fishes other than goldfish, so after a brief review of the most commonly seen goldfish varieties, a small gallery of suitable starter species is included to help you make the right choice.

Your aquarium will continue to delight and surprise you. However, sometimes things do not run smoothly and unexpected problems can arise. Providing you tackle these promptly, you can usually overcome them. We look at how to keep your fish in good health and how to encourage them to breed.

The importance of regular aquarium maintenance cannot be too highly stressed. We look at how to keep all your equipment running efficiently. It makes sense to have a supply of spares such as airpump diaphragms, fluorescent tubes and perhaps a standby heater, as problems demanding immediate attention invariably arise when your aquatic store is closed!

If you are completely new to fishkeeping, we are confident that your coldwater aquarium will be just the start of a growing involvement within the hobby. You will meet friendly folk, perhaps join an aquatic club and realise how many more exciting challenges await you. Your first tank is rarely your last!

Each type of filtration has its advantages and drawbacks relating to cost, efficiency in a given situation or the type of fish kept. Some are simple and straightforward, for use in hospital or fry-rearing tanks, for example. Others are more complex, as they are designed to support a well-stocked tank without the need for too much maintenance.

Undergravel filters

In this type of filter, the gravel substrate itself acts as the filter medium. Beneath it is a single perforated plate covering the tank base. Alternatively, smaller plates interlock to form the base grid. At one or both rear corners of the plate is an uplift tube. In the air-powered version, an airline from the pump is attached to an airstone lowered down the tube. Another version feeds an air supply from the pump direct to the base of the tube.

The airlift effect draws water up the tube, and as levels must remain constant, the tank contents are constantly drawn down through the perforated plates and through the substrate, where beneficial bacteria purify harmful waste. These filters also act mechanically, pulling particles out of suspension. Eventually the substrate will become blocked, but regular use of a gravel cleaner will prevent this happening for a year or more.

In the powered version, a small pump known as a powerhead is fitted into the top of the uplift tube and the impeller draws water up the tube, returning it in a powerful jet. Some models have a venturi feature, in which a small tube draws in air from above the surface and mixes it with the outflow.

Left: If you choose an undergravel filter, you must fit the plates and uplifts at the bottom of the tank before the substrate goes in. Do not force them. This is a modular filter plate that slots together. The thinner, all-in-one type may need to be trimmed with scissors.

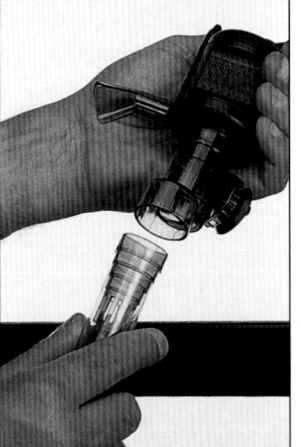

Left: This powerhead fits via an adapter into the undergravel uplift tube. To reduce turbulence, direct the return flow against the back glass of the tank. This versatile model can be rotated, even when fitted in the tank.

Above: A powerhead connected to the undergravel plate via an uplift tube. You may need to shorten the tube so that the motor is submerged to the correct level. Note the venturi tube at the top to draw air into the water return.

Box filters

Inexpensive air-powered box filters are fine on their own for small tanks, and particularly handy for gently filtering breeding, fry-rearing and quarantine systems, all of which need to be kept basic and easy to service. The media will soon become colonised by bacteria, and the filter then acts mechanically and biologically. There is no better way to mature a new tank than to add one of these small filters that has been kept running elsewhere. Change the filter floss and activated carbon granules when the flow rate slows down, but retain the ceramic media after giving it a gentle rinse through.

Below: You can ballast a simple box filter with gravel, marbles or ceramic cylinders (as here). On top of this is a 'sandwich' of filter floss with activated carbon in a nylon stocking. Carbon takes out impurities, but do not use it if you are adding chemical medications to the water.

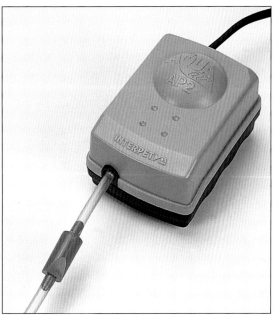

Above: A single-outlet airpump is the powerhouse for both these filters. Note the one-way check valve in the connecting airline, which prevents water back-siphoning into the pump if the electrical supply is turned off or fails.

Gang valves

Gang valves are useful for diverting a single air supply to two or more pieces of equipment. They stick unobtrusively to the back of the tank with an adhesive pad. Brass or stainless steel valves will last longer than plastic. Plain 'T' or 'X' pieces are not recommended, as air takes the line of least resistance and it is almost impossible to achieve a balance.

Sponge filters

These air-powered filters come into their own in fry-rearing tanks, as the occupants cannot be sucked into the mechanism. Microorganisms that colonise the easily-removable foam cartridges provide live food for fishes at a time when they need it most. The foam gathers dirt particles and also acts biologically.

Above: Sponge filters can also be the primary means of filtration where space is limited, or in hospital or breeding tanks. In twin models like this one, clean the sponges alternately as they begin to block, so there is always one with a healthy bacterial population.

Often, aquatic shops will sell real or artificial rocks under trade names that give no clue to what they really are. You must investigate further before putting them into your tank. Most are safe, but a few are suitable only for marine set-ups: others may be too rough or sharp-edged. Be wary of rocks with a very soft outline, which suggests that they are water-soluble. Pieces with crevices need thorough washing to remove deep-seated dirt, or even insects which may have crept inside. If you suspect that a piece of rock is high in calcium carbonate, use the acid test shown on this page.

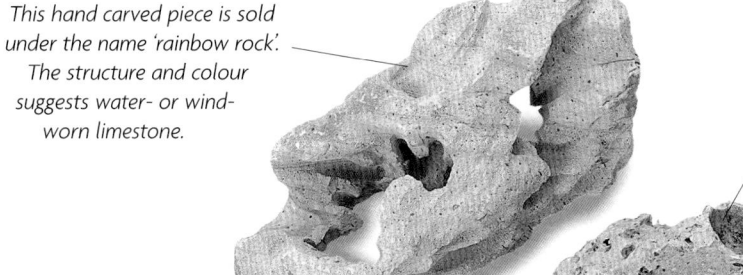

This hand carved piece is sold under the name 'rainbow rock'. The structure and colour suggests water- or wind-worn limestone.

This is so-called 'ocean rock'. Be sure to test it before use to check if it will raise the pH levels in the tank.

Below: Avoid any rocks such as tufa or marble that are high in calcium carbonate, as these can raise the pH level. Test any suspect materials with rust-removing liquid or gel, which contains phosphoric acid. If the rock fizzes, do not use it. Be careful and wash off all traces of the chemical before the rockwork goes into the tank.

Grotto ceramic is a manmade rock, inert and able to support good bacteria in its porous structure.

Rocks showing more than one colour can be dramatic. This is pink, with veins of quartz. Caution! Carry out the acid test before use.

Granite is safe, but rather stark and angular when broken into small pieces like this.

Sold as 'African rock', this red, striated piece of rock passes the acid test.

Novelty ornaments

All kinds of novelty ornaments are available for aquariums, including a 3-D shark that is held in place by magnets and seems to pierce the glass! Younger fishkeepers are particularly fascinated by animated air-operated ornaments, such as bubbling divers and opening treasure chests. These do have a practical function because they introduce extra aeration into the tank. They are very much a matter of taste.

Below: When you have decided where the rocks are to go, silicone them into place. Squeeze large beads of silicone onto any hard, clean surface. Fill any gaps with more silicone. Trim away any silicone that is visible once it is dry.

Glass decor can look very attractive when light shines through it. Try chunks of coloured glass or glass pebbles, or even well-washed antique bottles as shown here. These suggest the bottom of a river or canal through which boats have passed long ago!

Bamboo canes look good in a coldwater tank. String some together with nylon thread and push them into the substrate. Plug the ends with aquarium putty and when this is dry, apply two coats of clear polyurethane varnish to seal the bamboo. Remember to treat the ends, where the bamboo is at its most porous.

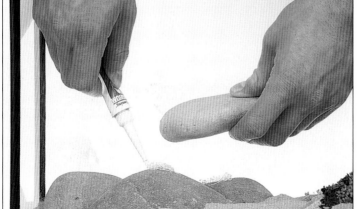

Hard coal is a jet-black shiny rock that looks good with a black gravel substrate. Scrub the pieces thoroughly before use to remove any dust. If the coal crumbles, reject it.

Coldwater setups in centrally heated rooms rarely fall below 18°C (64°F) and will support many plant species sold for tropical aquariums, such as straight vallis *(Vallisneria spiralis)*. However, temperature is not the only concern; soft-leaved plants are prone to being nibbled away by most of the fish species we are interested in, particularly goldfish. And unless they have strong, established root systems, natural plants will be dislodged by the larger tank occupants. The plants featured on these pages are undemanding and easy to replace if damaged by the fishes. Always buy true aquatic plants and not small specimens of houseplants, which will live for only a few weeks before rotting away.

Planting vallisneria

Put each plant in singly. Wind the roots around your index finger, make a depression in the gravel with your middle finger and gently manoeuvre the roots into position. Leave the crowns clear of the substrate or they may rot.

Apple-green myriophyllum grows tall, but pinching out the tips keeps it compact. A good oxygenating plant.

Vallisneria spiralis (straight vallis) produces straplike leaves. It is an ideal background plant, propagated by runners.

Right: *These goldfish are clearly at home swimming among the fine leaves of Elodea canadensis, a robust plant that will thrive in a coldwater aquarium.*

54

Other plants for a temperate aquarium

All these plants are suitable for slightly warmer tanks where the temperature does not fall below 18°C/64°F for any length of time. They are unlikely to survive the attentions of goldfish, but smaller fishes will not bother them.

Aponogeton ulvaceus *has beautiful, broad, wavy leaves.*

Crassula helmsii *is a small-leaved, thicket-forming plant.*

Didiplis diandra *(water hedge) forms low thickets.*

Echinodorus tenellus *(pygmy chain swordplant) is an ideal groundcover plant that spreads by runners.*

Eleocharis acicularis *(hairgrass) is suitable for foreground planting.*

Hydrocotyle verticillata *(pennywort) has circular leaves formed atop long stems.*

Lilaeopsis novae-zelandiae *(New Zealand grass) forms thickets. It is a good middle-ground plant.*

Nymphoides aquatica *(banana plant). An oddity, throwing pale, wavy leaves from a woody tuber.*

Rotala macrandra 'Florida' *(red rotala). This bushy, narrow-leaved plant is easy to propagate by top cuttings.*

Left: Bacopa caroliniana *(baby's tears) has small, fleshy leaves. It is ideal for the hard-water environment of a typical coldwater setup. The stems are delicate; take off the lowest pair of leaves before pushing cuttings into the gravel.*

Hygrophila polysperma *(dwarf hygrophila) is an inexpensive stem plant, readily propagated by top cuttings.*

Cryptocoryne willisii *has leathery leaves growing in flat rosettes. In good light it will form dense thickets, in poor light it becomes rather spindly.*

Right: Sagittaria pusilla *(dwarf sagittaria) forms carpets and puts out runners. The closely-related* Sagittaria subulata *is a native North American plant with finer leaves, growing 30cm (12in) tall. Specimens from their country of origin will be hardier than Asian-grown imports.*

Lobelia cardinalis *has dark green to reddish leaves and responds well to trimming back. This relatively slow grower can be propagated by stem cuttings or started from seed sown in trays of damp potting mix.*

Other suitable plants for a coldwater tank

Armoracia aquatica *(American watercress) has two distinct leaf forms: rounded at first, and later rather fernlike. Propagate from the aerial shoots growing from the flower stem.*

Echinodorus osiris *from southern South America is one of the few swordplants that will thrive in cool water (down to 10°C/50°F). This ideal background plant bears lance-shaped leaves, reddish bronze when young, on longish stems. Do not cover the crown with substrate as it will rot. Propagate the plantlets that grow from the flower stem. Other suitable swordplants are* Echinodorus horemanii *and* E. uruguayensis.

Lysimachia nummularia *is a stem plant with tiny, rounded leaves. Kept well trimmed, it makes a good foreground plant that branches thickly. A golden form is also available.*

Saururus cernuus *(lizard tail) has broad, heart-shaped leaves and a fairly low growth habit.*

There are several species of ludwigia suitable for a coldwater aquarium. The leaves of red ludwigia (L. mullerti) are reddish underneath and provide a useful colour contrast.

Hydrocotyle (pennywort) moves attractively in the current. It is not a dense plant and suitable for all areas of the tank.

Cabomba caroliniana *is a prolific and inexpensive aquarium plant. The whorls of fine foliage create attractive patterns under tank lights.*

Right: Ceratophyllum demersum *(hornwort) is a rootless, branching plant with whorls of fine leaves. It grows very rapidly, providing cover for fish, and is an excellent spawning medium. Propagate it from side shoots cut from the main stem.*

Goldfish for your aquarium

By far the commonest beginner's choice for the coldwater aquarium is the goldfish – and with good reason! It is hardy, long-lived, tolerant of a wide range of water chemistry and temperatures and freely available around the world.

Goldfish (Carassius auratus) were domesticated by the Chinese during the Sung Dynasty (960-1279 A.D.), and by the fourteenth century were being kept in ceramic bowls as household pets. Most of the numerous 'fancy' varieties have been developed in the Far East by the Chinese and the Japanese. Amazingly, all these exotic creatures share common ancestry and carry the same scientific name.

The cheapest and most trouble-free starter goldfish is the common, or standard, type, with normal scalation, fins, eyes and body shape. The greater the variation from the norm, the more

delicate the fish is likely to be, and tankmates must be chosen with care. Normally, all goldfish are compatible with one another, but problems can arise if slow-moving, long-finned varieties are mixed with other species. Watch out for signs of bullying, eye-worrying and fin-nipping.

The more 'extreme' fancy goldfish, such as bubble-eyes and celestials, are really only for the specialist. Fluid-filled eye sacs can be damaged on sharp gravel or attacked by other fishes, while goldfish lacking a dorsal fin may swim laboriously and not be able to obtain their fair share at feeding time.

Common goldfish - *Carassius auratus*

The world's most popular pet, the common goldfish, is a typically 'carp-shaped' metallic red or orange fish with paired pectoral and ventral fins and single dorsal, anal and caudal (tail) fins. It can grow to 50cm (20in) in the wild, but remains much smaller in the aquarium. Young specimens often show black markings that later fade. Common goldfish are famously hardy, but should be treated with the same respect as all other varieties. They are good feeders and active swimmers, and deserve more space than the traditional goldfish bowl can offer.

Stocking levels

Coldwater aquariums are not as efficient as tropical setups at breaking down waste products, so this 60x 38x30cm (24x15x12in) tank will support a maximum of 30cm (12in) of fish, excluding tails. That could mean 12 2.5cm (1in)-long fishes, six 5cm (2in) fishes or four 7.5cm (3in) fishes. But you must make allowance for growth. With goldfish, that means halving the total fish length to 15cm (6in). You may wish to keep smaller species, such as White Cloud Mountain minnows (Tanichthys albonubes), bought as adults or juveniles, in which case you can stock closer to the eventual limit in those first weeks.

Shubunkin (London and Bristol)

The shubunkin is another popular single-tailed variety. These fish lack the guanine pigment in and beneath the scales, so that their skin appears matt. They are also calico (multicoloured) fishes. The London shubunkin is similar in shape to the common goldfish, but with rounded ends to the tail. The Bristol shubunkin is longer-bodied, with more developed fins and a squared-off tail. Both types can be boisterous to less active tankmates.

Comet goldfish

The comet is similar to the common goldfish, but slimmer-bodied and with greatly elongated finnage, particularly the single tail. It was developed in the late nineteenth century in America. This fast and graceful swimmer needs plenty of tank space as it grows. The red and white sarasa comet, shown here, is particularly attractive. Many of today's farmed goldfish are of an intermediate form between the comet and common varieties.

Goldfish for your aquarium

▲ Moor

A matt black, veiltailed goldfish with double caudal and anal fins and a flaglike dorsal. The body is high-backed, while the eyes are large and protuberant. Like all short-bodied goldfish varieties, moors can be prone to swimbladder trouble unless fed live food, such as daphnia, which has a high roughage content. Despite their exotic appearance, moors are not particularly delicate and contrast well with the more colourful goldfish varieties.

▽ Oranda

Orandas are short-bodied fish with long, paired finnage, a high dorsal fin and a characteristic hood growth on the head. There are several types, including calico, blue, brown and the red-cap, with a white body and red head. They are sedate swimmers, but you will need a deep tank (45cm/18in or more in depth) for larger specimens.

Other varieties of fancy goldfish

New varieties of fancy goldfish are being developed all the time, but these examples are well established in the hobby.

Right: The ranchu is the Japanese form of the lionhead. The characteristic head hood can also cover the cheeks and gill plates – the four-lobed tail is held stiffly. There is no dorsal fin.

Below: A white ryukin. Good examples should have a short body, a high back and fairly long finnage, held extended as here. The tail is deeply divided, with four lobes, and there are twin anal fins.

Right: 'Telescope eyes' are found on many fancy goldfish varieties, but should not be confused with the disease condition known as 'pop-eye', or exophthalmus, associated with dropsy. This is a telescope-eyed fantail.

Japanese rice fish - *Oryzias latipes*

For aquariums where the temperature does not fall below 18°C (64°F), this little fish has a lot going for it. It grows to only 3.5cm (1.4in) and is undemanding about diet, providing there is some variation from flake food. Colour is usually white and orange, with silvery scales to the rear of the body. After spawning, females carry clusters of eggs around the vent, which they later wipe onto plants. These fish are best kept with tankmates of a similar size.

Shiner - *Notropis lutrensis*

A home-grown fish for US hobbyists, and commonly imported into Europe, this shoaling member of the carp family grows to only 9cm (3.5in) and is as undemanding as the goldfish in its feeding requirements and husbandry. It is happy in water down to 15°C (59°F), but prefers well-filtered tanks with a good water flow to mimic its natural stream habitat. Males are more colourful and thickset than females.

White Cloud Mountain minnow *Tanichthys albonubes*

These hardy little fishes from Southern China are happiest in the temperature range 18-22°C (64-72°F) provided by most coldwater aquariums. They show their brightest colours when kept in shoals, and will eat live, frozen or flake foods. They are easy to spawn in planted tanks, but the fry are unlikely to escape being eaten in a community setup. The males are the slimmer and more colourful fishes. White Clouds occupy the middle and upper layers of the water and grow to a manageable 4cm (1.6in).

Three-spined stickleback
Gasterosteus aculeatus

Known in some areas as the 'tiddler', this little fish grows to just 12cm (4.5in) and is worth keeping in a single-species tank with sandy substrate for its interesting breeding behaviour. The male develops a red belly and builds a nest of plant material into which he lures a succession of females and then fertilises the eggs. He guards these and the subsequent fry. Our 60cm (24in) tank will house a single male and four or five females. Males can be quite aggressive at spawning time. The natural food of these fishes consists of small aquatic invertebrates, but captive sticklebacks will sometimes take freeze-dried mosquito larvae or flake. They are tolerant of a wide temperature range of 4-18°C (39-64°F).

Weather loach
Misgurnus anguillicaudatus

The common name of this comical, bewhiskered fish stems from its habit of swimming wildly up and down the aquarium when atmospheric pressure falls just before a thunderstorm. At other times it is quite secretive, and needs a tank with plenty of cover. A fine substrate into which to dig in search of food suits this loach best. Unfortunately, plants can be uprooted, too. The weather loach can grow to a maximum length of 50cm (20in), but this is rarely attained in the aquarium. An albino form is also available in the hobby.

Foods and feeding

Captive fishes are entirely dependent on their owner for food, which must be offered regularly and in a varied form to mimic as closely as possible what would be available in the wild. Most coldwater aquarium fishes are cyprinids (members of the carp family), which means they are omnivorous. Their diet includes small aquatic invertebrates, land-dwelling insects blown onto the water and a certain amount of vegetable matter.

A good-quality flake food for goldfish will contain all these elements, plus added vitamins and minerals and perhaps a colour-enhancer. But to keep your fishes in peak condition, alternate this staple diet with other prepared or safe live food items, which are featured on these pages.

Daphnia (water fleas)

Brineshrimp

Left: *Aquatic live foods include mosquito larvae and pupae, daphnia and bloodworms. These can be safely collected from the wild, providing the pond in question does not contain fish. Live tubifex are best avoided, as they inhabit polluted mud, but the freeze-dried alternative is safe.*

Stick-on tablets

Bloodworms (midge larvae of a blood-red colour)

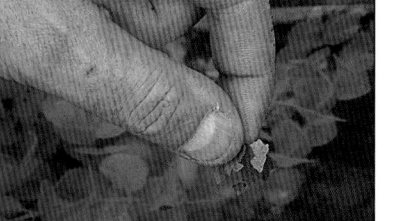

Above: *Because a tub of flake is so convenient to use, it is all too easy to overfeed, so be sparing. Once your fish become accustomed to you, they will take individual flakes from your fingers.*

Freeze-dried bloodworm

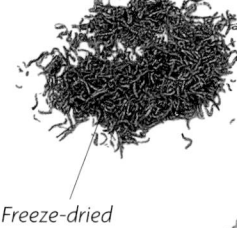

Sinking granules for bottom-feeding fish.

Freeze-dried tubifex cubes

Flakes are available in herbivore, carnivore and general formulae.

Making a wormery

Earthworms, chopped or fed whole, are protein-packed and excellent for conditioning parent fish before they spawn. To collect your own worms, dig over a shady corner of the garden and cover a patch of soil with one or two hessian sacks. Keep these well-watered and seed them with all your used teabags and soft food scraps. Worms will congregate under the sacks and can be picked off the surface – much easier than spadework! Whiteworms, grindalworms and microworms (relished by growing fry) can all be bought as cultures. They are a useful livefood standby during winter.

Right: Freeze-dried foods include cubes of tubifex, which stick to the aquarium glass, as shown here. The goldfish can be seen in the background circling with anticipation of the meal! Individually dried mosquito larvae suit surface-feeding fishes, as they are quite buoyant. Tablet foods can also be stuck to the glass or left to sink, when they will be fed on by bottom-dwelling fish such as the weather loaches.

Holiday feeding

Healthy adult coldwater fish will happily go without food for a week or two, although you may find they have dined on natural plants in your absence. If you are away for longer than that, package up daily rations of flake or freeze-dried food in a twist of foil and leave them in the fridge for a friend, neighbour or relative to administer. Hide the tub of flake in case your helper is tempted to give the fish a bit extra. Alternatively, invest in an autofeeder – a timer-controlled reservoir for flake or small granules – and programme it to dispense one or more meals daily.

Below: This battery-operated autofeeder is easy to programme to dispense two meals per day. At the preset times, the food compartment rotates and the contents drop into the tank. Adjust the blue wheel to control the feed quantity.

When to feed your fish

Overfeeding is a common mistake with beginners, who think that whenever their fish come eagerly to the front of the tank they must be hungry. The filtration system of a coldwater aquarium can easily be overloaded if you ladle in too much food. The fish may eat most of it, but will only partially digest it, shedding more waste products into the water. One meal a day is quite sufficient; it is far better for your fish to be hungry than

obese. Allow yourself time to watch them feeding. Give them only as much dried or frozen food as they will consume in 10-15 minutes. If you keep herbivores, leave green foods, such as lettuce or courgettes, in the tank and replenish them daily with fresh supplies. Make sure that all the fish in your aquarium are getting their share. Offer them a mixed menu of floating and sinking items of different particle sizes.

Fresh frozen irradiated foods

These are sold as individual portions in foil-sealed trays. Simply pop one out and drop it into the tank, where it quickly defrosts.

When defrosted, one cube of frozen bloodworms provides a good 'meaty' meal for larger or spawning fishes.

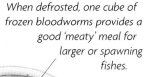

Although goldfish will breed readily in an outdoor pond, the chances of this happening in a 60cm (24in) aquarium are slim. Even if you have mature males and females and they spawn, any fertile eggs will soon be eaten by the parents or other inhabitants of the tank.

This holds true for most of the carp family, which do not give birth to live young but deposit their eggs on the leaves of aquatic plants. On hatching, the fry are tiny and helpless. To survive and grow, they require protection from predators and specialist feeding on minute organisms, neither of which is possible in a display aquarium containing adult fish.

Setting up a breeding tank

As your hobby progresses, you may wish to breed your goldfish. For this you will need one, and preferably two, additional tanks with a minimum volume of 90 litres (20 gallons). It is best to start with common goldfish, as it is easier than with round-bodied varieties to see when the female is carrying eggs. She will become noticeably plump.

Below: In this pair of redcap orandas, the male (left) shows tubercles on his gill covers, indicating that he is in spawning condition. Do not expect eggs to survive in a community tank; the parents and other fishes will eat them.

Sexually mature males sometimes develop spawning tubercles (pinhead-sized white lumps) on the gill covers and the leading edges of the pectoral fins, and their skin will become rough to the touch.

The spawning process

Early summer is the best time to attempt a spawning. House the parents in a 90-136 litre (20-30 gallon) unfurnished, filtered tank, separated down the middle by a divider and sited in a quiet corner that receives the sun first thing in the morning. Feed the fish nutritious conditioning foods, including chopped earthworms, for at least a week. Then remove the divider and add a spawning medium, such as a mop made from strands of nylon wool tied to a cork.

Spawning should take place early the next morning as the sun's rays strike the tank. The eggs will adhere to the mop. Remove the parent goldfish immediately and add a heater set to 21°C (70°F). The fry will hatch in three to four days and will require feeding two days later, when they have absorbed their yolk sacs. The easiest first food is a liquid preparation for egglaying fishes. After a fortnight, the fry can be weaned onto newly-hatched brineshrimp, followed by crumbled flake. Bear in mind that a single spawning can result in up to 1000 eggs and unless you have many tanks or a pond, it will be impossible to raise all the youngsters.

If you lack space, it is still possible to breed your fish, but be selective. Instead of keeping a mixed community, try a species tank holding only one type of fish. Three-spined sticklebacks *(Gasterosteus aculeatus)* are a good choice; keep one male and

three or four females. The tank should have a fine substrate and plenty of fine plant matter with which the male constructs a domed nest. He lures females inside one by one and the eggs are laid and fertilised. He will guard the eggs and fry, but it is best to remove the females as soon as they have spawned, as males are quite protective of their brood.

Other small fish that exhibit brood care are the bullhead *(Cottus gobio)* and the rosy minnow *(Pimephales promelas)*. Provide a tank with sand and shingle, plus rocks or half-flowerpots, which the fish will use as spawning caves.

Raising fry

The fry of goldfish and other coldwater species are prone to disease unless their rearing tank is spacious and kept spotlessly clean. The floor of a bare aquarium is easier to siphon clean than one with a substrate and fussy decor, which can trap fry and harbour uneaten food. Use a sponge filter, which will not draw tiny fish inside, and a heater set to a temperature of 21°C (70°F).

Perform regular partial water changes with water brought up to tank temperature, and use your test kits to keep a check on water quality. The difficult part of the process is to keep the fry well fed without polluting the tank. Unlike adult fish, they will need several small feeds a day. You can see if they are getting enough by their rounded bellies.

Culturing live foods for fry is a hobby in itself. Well before you plan a spawning, set up several brineshrimp hatcheries to run in rotation so that the newly-hatched larvae, called *Artemia* nauplii, are always in supply. Do the same with microworm and grindalworm cultures.

Infusoria are an ideal first food. Grow the microorganisms by pouring boiling water into a glass jar over hay or banana skins and leave the culture to stand for several days. The water will go cloudy before clearing again, and the infusoria, which appear as opaque patches against the light, can then be fed via a pipette or eye dropper.

As the fry grow, the danger of overcrowding in the aquarium increases. Retain only the most colourful or interesting young fish and humanely dispose of any that show deformities (see page 69). If you are breeding fancy goldfish, only a small percentage are likely be good examples of their variety.

Above: *Liquid fry food for egglayers is a specialist diet for newly-hatched fish that are too small even to take powdered dried food. It contains microorganisms in suspension. Squeeze the plastic bottle and drip the food into the tank.*

Left: *These 48 hour-old shubunkin fry are still not free swimming and would be quickly eaten in a tank containing any adult fishes.*

Starting off with healthy stock is essential, so choose your fish with care. Bear in mind that they are probably more seasoned travellers than you are! Popular coldwater fishes are mass-produced on farms in the Far East, Europe and America, and at every stage of the long journey to the retailer they are subjected to handling and repacking, with changes in water temperature and chemistry. Inevitably, some losses occur in transit.

A quarantine or hospital tank

Having finally reached the shop, the fishes will need time to recuperate, even though there may be nothing visibly wrong with them. Good retailers will have quarantine tanks away from the main shop area, ready for the new arrivals, whereas poor ones will put them on sale immediately, laying fish health problems at your door, not theirs!

When selecting fish, choose only active specimens that are swimming normally with spread

Get to know your fish

Record the behaviour patterns of your fish, as any departures from the norm could spell trouble. For example, if fish are gasping at the surface, they could be short of oxygen. In this case, step up aeration with an airstone and check the flow through your filter, which may have become clogged with dirt. Also watch out for fish that skulk alone in one corner of the tank or hide away behind plants and decor. This is usually a sign of stress or ill-health.

fins, and showing good colour. Check for ulcers on the belly region, badly split fins which could be the site of future bacterial or fungal infections, thin bellies or sunken eyes. Fish hiding away in a corner are suspect. If even one individual in a sales tank is sick, leave the rest alone, as many fish diseases and parasites are infectious or contagious.

Setting up a quarantine/hospital tank
As a beginner, with only one tank and no quarantine facility, you must rely on your retailer to sell you healthy stock. Later, you may decide on a second aquarium for new arrivals, and this can double as a hospital tank. It need not be a complex setup; just provide the bare essentials to give the fish shelter and purify the water. Use a matured sponge or box filter. Include a low-wattage heater, as some medications work best at raised temperatures. There is no need for a hood or lighting, but cover the tank with a sheet of glass to stop the fish jumping out.

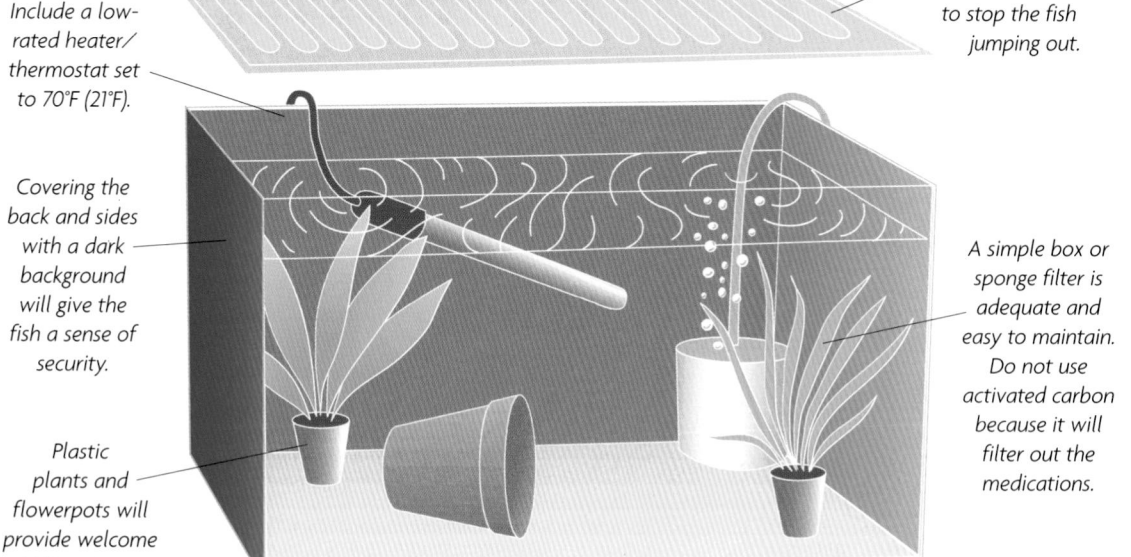

Include a low-rated heater/thermostat set to 70°F (21°F).

Covering the back and sides with a dark background will give the fish a sense of security.

Plastic plants and flowerpots will provide welcome hiding places.

Fit a cover to prevent contamination and to stop the fish jumping out.

A simple box or sponge filter is adequate and easy to maintain. Do not use activated carbon because it will filter out the medications.

Sometimes it is best to isolate a sick fish and give it individual treatment. This would apply in cases of dropsy or bacterial ulceration, where the condition might otherwise spread to other fish. An outbreak of the white spot parasite, however, will include free-swimming and encysted stages, as well as the visible spots. Treating the main tank with a proprietary remedy over the recommended period is the only way to eliminate all stages and prevent reinfestation.

Coping with health problems

Most health problems in coldwater fishes are easy to diagnose and treat, providing they are caught early. It is important to know which are brought about by pathogens (disease-causing organisms) and which are the result of congenital defects, such as a defective swimbladder, for which there is no long-term cure.

The availability of veterinary antibiotics varies in different countries. In most cases, antibiotics will not be necessary, but you do need to be sure what is wrong with your fish before rushing out to buy a 'cure' that may not work. Follow the instructions to the letter, ensuring you know the exact volume of your tank, otherwise you may under- or overdose. Give the product time to work and do not stop the treatment before it has run its course.

Some fish species, notably orfe and rudd, are sensitive to certain medications. This information should be on the label, but if in doubt, do not administer them.

Do not use fish medications past their sell-by date. At best, they will be less effective and at worst they can actually become toxic over time. Store them in a cool, dark place, away from children, and never mix cures unless you know the combination to be safe; a lethal chemical reaction may take place.

Disposing of fish humanely

If a sick fish is beyond saving, the best thing is to dispose of it humanely. If you can bring yourself to do it, the quickest method is to sever the spinal cord behind the head with a sharp knife. Alternatively, obtain the fish anaesthetic MS222 from a veterinary surgeon or pharmacist and leave the patient in a solution of this for several hours. Never flush a fish down the lavatory, throw it on the floor or place it alive in the freezer. Freezing affects the capillary blood vessels just under the skin, causing the fish great pain before it loses consciousness.

New tank syndrome

The commonest health pitfall – and one that occurs in the early stages of running in an aquarium – arises from being in too much of a hurry to stock it with fish. This 'new tank syndrome' is more accurately known as ammonia or nitrite poisoning and can be avoided by frequent water testing and carrying out partial water changes. Other problems develop more slowly. Even when the aquarium is established, missing out on water changes can lead to a build-up of nitrate which, although not very toxic, will stress the fish and lower their resistance to disease.

Left: *A bacterial ulcer, accompanied by reddening of the area around it and the beginning of raised scales. This fish will almost certainly require antibiotics for a complete recovery.*

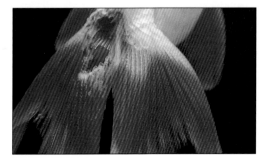

Right: *Bacterial finrot on the tail of an oranda. The fin rays and connective tissue are clearly eroded, but if treated before the infection reaches the tail root, the fish may survive. Use an aquarium bactericide.*

Above: *A fish louse (Argulus) attached near the tail of this goldfish. You can carefully pick off individual parasites with tweezers and treat the aquarium water with a proprietary medication.*

Regular maintenance is essential to keep your fish and plants healthy and your tank looking good. Most tasks take only a few minutes and should be seen as a pleasure, not a chore. It is impossible to lay down a set schedule, as tank needs vary according to how many fish they contain and what species, and the type of filtration used. Start by working out a maintenance timetable of daily, weekly or two-weekly, monthly and occasional jobs. With the help of an aquarium log, you will soon be able to adapt these to your setup, and if anything goes wrong, you may only need to rethink what needs attending to and when. Often, subtle behaviour changes in your fish are the first clue that something is amiss.

With any job that involves putting your hands into the tank, be sure to turn off all electrical equipment at the main supply first. If you have a heater, leave it unplugged for 10 minutes to cool down before lowering the water level, or it may be damaged.

If your siphon incorporates a gravel cleaner, push the rigid end into the substrate, where it will draw up light debris. If you use an undergravel filter, do not vacuum the gravel too deeply or you will lose most of the beneficial bacteria.

The importance of water changes

Water changes are essential to dilute pollutants, particularly nitrates. Real plants will help keep levels down, but are not the complete answer, as coldwater fishes generate a lot of solid waste that must not be allowed to build up on the floor of the tank or go into solution.

You will need a plain light-coloured plastic bucket (reserved for aquarium use) and a siphoning device. This can be either a simple length of clear wide-bore plastic tubing or a more sophisticated piece of equipment with a self-starter. Stand the bucket on the floor, place the free end of the tube into the tank and start the siphoning action. Watch that you do not suck up small fish or gravel or bruise plant leaves, and do not overfill the bucket or you will splash the carpet as you carry it away for emptying. (Old aquarium water contains at least some nitrate and so is ideal for feeding houseplants).

With a little practice, you will be able to siphon out dirt at the same time as you conduct a partial water change of between 10 and 20%. This is also the time to remove algae from the tank glass with a magnet or scraper and tidy up your plants, removing dead or damaged leaves.

Top-up water should preferably be drawn off and left to stand overnight to bring it up to room temperature. This interval will also help chlorine to dissipate. If this is not possible, spray water from the tap into your bucket and then add a water conditioner to neutralise any remaining chlorine or chloramine.

Then, using your thermometer as a check, add boiled water from a kettle until the top-up supply is at tank temperature.

Do not pour the new water violently into the tank as you will disturb the decor and upset the fishes. Introduce it gently with a jug or, if you have somewhere high to stand the bucket, siphon it in slowly. Wipe the cover glass or plastic condensation tray clean of salts, which otherwise reduce the penetration of light into the tank, and while you have the hood open, check the watertight end caps on the fluorescent tube for tightness and give the reflector (if fitted) a wipe with a clean cloth.

Below: Use only a clean, damp cloth to wipe the condensation tray. Plastic trays will not last forever, and scratch easily. The moment they start to become opaque, replace them.

Cleaning filters

Biological filters should run 24 hours a day to support the colonies of beneficial (aerobic) bacteria that break down aquarium toxins into relatively harmless nitrate (see the nitrogen cycle on page 26).

The usual sign that internal or external power filters need cleaning is a fall-off in flow rate, caused by partial blockage of the mechanical media inside. If you do not attend to this, water will take the easiest line of resistance and parts of the media will become deoxygenated and foul as the good bacteria are replaced by anaerobic bugs. Use your nose to detect this. Instead of a healthy, rich, earthy odour, the filter will smell like rotten eggs.

Fortunately, this rarely happens, unless the filter has been switched off for several hours, and your cleaning routine will restore full flow and efficiency. Never use neat tapwater or detergents to clean filters, as chemicals will destroy the bacteria. The best water is that drawn from your tank; otherwise use boiled and cooled water from the kettle.

Undergravel filters

After several years' constant use, undergravel filters will clog with dirt and the tank will need to be stripped right down to access the filter plates for cleaning. However, this drastic measure can be delayed indefinitely by regular use of a gravel cleaner. These can be air- or battery-powered, work on water pressure from the tap or operate on a simple siphon principle. Water and

Right: Testing the water for nitrite level is a vital part of routine maintenance. This test involves adding a tablet to a sample of tank water in a tube, shaking it vigorously and comparing the colour change to a printed chart.

Below: The more care you take in setting up your aquarium, the easier it will be to keep it looking good. The healthy balance between fish and plants in this tank means that it will require only simple, regular maintenance for long-term success.

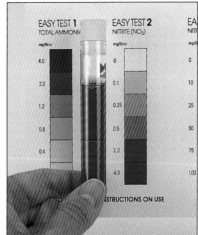

Regular maintenance

Daily
Remove uneaten food
Check the health of the fish
Check the water
    temperature
Check equipment (filters,
    lights, airpump)

Weekly/every two weeks
Make a 20-25% partial
    water change
Test for pH and nitrite level
Clean front glass of algae
Remove dead plant matter
    and vacuum substrate
    with a gravel cleaner
Clean cover glass or
    condensation tray

Monthly/as required
Clean filter and replace
    expendable media if
    necessary

Every 6-12 months
Service airpump and
    filter/powerhead motors
Replace lighting tubes
Replace airstones and
    airline
Scrub rocks/bogwood and
    plastic plants to remove
    build-up of algae

the top layer of gravel are drawn up a rigid, transparent tube. At a certain point, the substrate falls back under its own weight, but light debris carries on through and is either trapped in a mesh bag or flows to waste.

The siphon-action cleaner is the cheapest and best option. It allows you to combine cleaning the gravel with a partial water change, rather than return strained water to the tank.

Do not disturb the filter bed too deeply, as you risk destroying many of the bacteria it contains. If the flow through an air-operated undergravel filter reduces, it may be that a clogged airstone needs replacing. Also check that the delivery airline has not become partially blocked by a build-up of salts. If it has, replace it with fresh tubing.

Air-powered box filters

Remove the filter from the tank, discard the dirtiest filter floss and replace it with fresh. Activated carbon is best replenished every three months or so. Check that the feeder airline has not become blocked with debris. Lightly rinse ceramic media or ballast gravel in tank water and wipe the intake slats on the filter body clean of slime and algae.

Air-operated sponge filters

Remove the sponge (foam) from the manifolds and rinse it gently in old tank water. If there is more than one sponge, stagger the washing at two-weekly intervals, so that one is always clean and the other partially dirty. Eventually these relatively fine sponges will lose their elasticity and need replacing.

Cleaning an internal filter

1 Turn off the electricity supply. Unplug and remove the filter from its suckers or cradle and lift it vertically into a bowl or bucket into which you have siphoned about 2.5-5cm (1-2in) of tank water. Separate the motor from the canister, which can be left in the bowl.

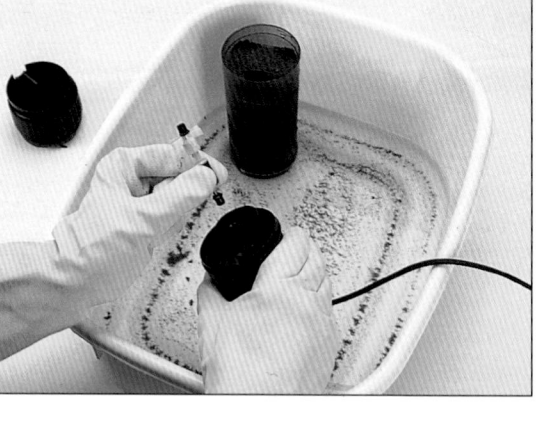

2 Remove the impeller and shaft and clean off the slime. Check the bearings for excessive play and replace them if necessary. Wipe inside the impeller housing with a clean, soft cloth. If the impeller sticks, remove the motor unit and give it a half turn with your finger to free it.

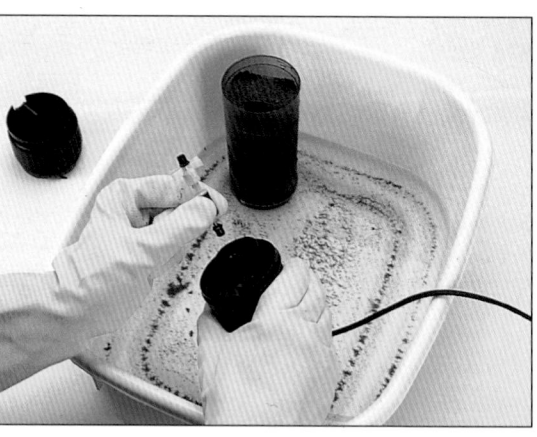

3 Remove the sponge and rinse it gently in the bowl. If there is more than one sponge, leave one dirty and clean the other, reversing the sequence next time so that there are always beneficial bacteria in the media. Reassemble the parts without forcing them and put the filter back.

Cleaning an external canister filter

1 Cleaning the external filter on the tank featured on pages 10-37 is an easy job, as this model is fitted with coupling taps. Turn these to the 'off' position and undo the plastic nuts securing the taps to the filter body. Place the filter in a shallow bowl and tilt it to drain off most of the water inside.

3 Remove the internal slatted basket by pulling the integral handle. Some filters have several modules that slot together to hold the different materials, but this is a one-piece assembly.

2 Remove the motor from the canister by releasing the locking tabs and pulling evenly until the two main components separate. Help will be appreciated here, as the 'O' ring assembly makes a tight fit. Take the impeller from its housing and clean it of slime and debris, wiping down all plastic parts with a damp cloth.

4 Remove the media from the slatted internal basket. Discard the soiled filter floss and exhausted activated carbon that we placed inside a nylon stocking.

5 Gently wash the permanent media, either foam pads or ceramic pieces. Loose-fill an old nylon stocking with fresh carbon and reassemble the media in the correct sequence with new filter floss on the top, as shown on page 17. Replace the motor unit, taking care to position it so that the locking tabs locate properly and the 'O' ring makes a seal all round the union. You may also need to clean the filter delivery pipes and spraybars of algae and slime, using a stiff bottlebrush' on a long, flexible wire handle. Couple the filter to the taps and turn them to the 'on' position. Water should siphon down into the canister, but if not, prime the filter according to the instructions.

Regular maintenance

Airpumps

Replace diaphragms every year or when they show signs of wear, whichever is the sooner. Impending failure (usually a split in the rubberised material) is signalled by reduced air output, noisy operation and/or undue vibration. Maintenance kits can include replacement flap valves. Fit these at the same time as new diaphragms.

Many airpumps contain a small air-filter pad located on the outside of the housing. Replace this when it becomes discoloured. Also check delivery airline for brittleness and ensure that one-way valves (if fitted) have not become clogged with dust.

Heater/thermostats

Apart from wiping the tube clear of salt deposits and occasionally replacing the suckers, these require no maintenance. Check that they are still working by brushing your hand against the tank as you go past and glancing at the thermometer. Heaters can fail in the 'on' as well as the 'off' position, so investigate an unduly high water temperature immediately. Have a replacement ready for emergencies.

Aquarium lights

Replace tubes every 12 months. Even if they still seem to be working normally, their useful light output will have diminished and this can affect plant growth. Keep tubes, reflectors and cover glasses dust-free. Check that endcaps on the starter unit have not perished or become brittle, that leads have not chafed against the hood and that plastic securing clips still grip the tubes tightly.

Above: Be sure to unplug your airpump before carrying out any regular maintenance. Here, the air filter pad is being replaced. The pump motor cover can be removed by unscrewing four corner screws beneath the housing.

Right: Service an airpump on a piece of pale-coloured cloth or paper, preferably at floor level so you do not drop and lose any components. Have all the spares to hand before you open the housing.

Servicing an airpump

Flap valves are held in place by hard rubber plugs.

Rubber sealing spacer

Electricity supply lead

Cover

The usual reason for an airpump failure is a split or perished diaphragm. Replace it every year.

Rubber pivot support

Air filter pad

Airline gets brittle and kinks. Replace it regularly.

Check the airstone. If this clogs, it will put back-pressure on the airpump, shortening its life.

Some essential spares

When you buy all your equipment, lay in a supply of spares so that you are not caught out at a time when the aquatic shop is closed. In addition to the spares shown here, also keep stocks of the following items: Test kit refills and medications for white spot, bacterial infections and fungus. Salt – useful against many minor ailments. A battery-operated airpump – useful in power cuts.

Airpump maintenance kit. Use all components at each service. (See page 74.)

Any old sponge will not do. These are open-cell filter foam inserts.

Heater/thermostats have uses, even in a coldwater tank. Keep a spare.

Silicone sealant – first aid for leaking tanks.

Rubber or plastic suckers for heaters and power filters

Brands of light tube come and go. Buy several of your favourite kind for continuity.

Airline. Buy in bulk.

Airstones. Discard when they start to block.

Filter floss is so cheap, there is no excuse for running out.

Activated carbon. Store in a dry place.

Essential spares for power filters vary between makes. Here are an impeller and 'O' rings.

You cannot have too many nets. To catch fish in the aquarium, you need two; and what about a small one to dip out dead plant leaves? Store nets wet, in a mild solution of aquarium disinfectant, and do not use them in more than one tank or you risk transmitting disease between them.

INDEX

Page numbers in **bold** indicate major entries; *italics* refer to captions and annotations; plain type indicates other text entries.

CREDITS

Practical photographs by Geoffrey Rogers
© Interpet Publishing.

The publishers would like to thank the
following photographers for providing
images, credited here by page number and
position: B(Bottom), T(Top), C(Centre),
BL(Bottom Left), etc.

Aaron Norman: 69(R)
Arend van den Nieuwenhuizen: Title page,
  48, 66
MP & C Piednoir/Aqua Press: 6, 8, 54(R),
  59(L), 61(BR), 69(C, Peter Cole), 69(BC),
  71(B)
Photomax (Max Gibbs): Credits page, 58,
  59(R), 60(L), 61(BL,TR), 62(CL,BC,TR), 63(B),
  67(B), 69(BR)
Mike Sandford: 63(T)

Artwork illustrations by Stuart Watkinson
© Interpet Publishing.

The publishers would like to thank Jason
Scott and all his staff at The Water Zoo, 439
Lincoln Road, Millfield, Peterborough PE1
2PE for providing space to photograph the
practical sequences. Thanks are also due to
Fosters Fires and Fuels, Heaver Tropics,
Hobby Fish Farm and Swallow Aquatics.

The information and recommendations in
this book are given without any guarantees
on the part of the author and publisher,
who disclaim any liability with the use of
this material.